# GOURMET

RECIPES FROM THE RED CENTRE

# pizzas

# GOURMET

## RECIPES FROM THE RED CENTRE

# pizzas

### GREGORY D. BOOCK & KIRK S. STUART

SIMON & SCHUSTER
AUSTRALIA

GOURMET PIZZAS

First published in Australasia in 1995 by
Simon & Schuster Australia
20 Barcoo Street, East Roseville NSW 2069

Viacom International
Sydney   New York   London   Toronto   Tokyo   Singapore

National Library of Australia
Cataloguing-in-Publication data

Boock, Greg and Stuart, Kirk.
    Gourmet pizzas : recipes from the Red Centre.

    Includes index.
    ISBN 0 7318 0485 6.

    1. Pizza. I. Red Centre. II. Title.

641.824

Photography by Stephen Stewart
Props supplied by Georgina Dolling Productions and
    Home & Garden on the Mall, Sydney
Design by Megan Smith
Printed in Malaysia by SNP Offset (M) SDN. BHD.

# Contents

~~~

# Acknowledgments

~~~

I WOULD LIKE TO ACKNOWLEDGE THE ASSISTANCE OF BUTTERFIELDS CHEESE FACTORS, WHO PROVIDED TECHNICAL SPECIFICATIONS ON ALL THE CHEESES USED THROUGHOUT THE BOOK.

THANKS ARE ALSO DUE TO MY VEGETABLE PROVIDORE, LEO, AT NORTHPOINT FRUIT, FOR THE ONGOING SUPPLY OF EXCELLENT PRODUCE, AT ANY TIME OF THE DAY, FOR THE PHOTOGRAPHIC SHOOT (EVEN IF WE DIDN'T USE IT IN THE FINAL SHOTS!).

AND THANK YOU TO THE EXCEPTIONALLY PATIENT AND CREATIVE FOOD STYLISTS, MEGAN AND SIOBHAN; THE PHOTOGRAPHER, STEPHEN; AND MY EDITOR, SIOBHAN.

LAST, AND CERTAINLY NOT LEAST, THANK YOU TO MY MUM, PATRICIA, FOR TREMENDOUS DEDICATION AND LOVE THROUGHOUT MY LIFE.

THE PUBLISHER WOULD LIKE TO THANK GEORGINA DOLLING PRODUCTIONS AND HOME & GARDEN ON THE MALL, SYDNEY, FOR THEIR GENEROSITY IN SUPPLYING PROPS FOR PHOTOGRAPHY.

# Introduction

History traces the origin of the pizza back to the Persian empire of 500 BC, when the Roman soldiers made camp bread containing locally available fruits and nuts. It is speculated that this style of bread bore a resemblance to what we now know as pizza.

It wasn't until the 1700s that peasant families in Naples, Italy, first began using tomatoes as a part of the topping. In fact, it was a local baker or pizzaiolo, Don Raffaele Esposito, who developed the infamous margherita combination in honour of the Queen's birthday. Using the colours of the flag for inspiration, he made a pizza with mozzarella, tomato and fresh basil.

Italian immigrants soon took the pizza to North America in the late 1800s and the first pizzeria was established in New York City in 1895. The pizza continued to snowball in popularity and it soon became a national, and then global, food item.

In the late 1980s, people became more aware of fats and cholesterol, and learned how to count calories. The results saw some inspiring chefs, such as Wolfgang Puck, reinterpret the modern pizza, making it a culinary delight by using exotic ingredients and cooking the pizzas in wood-fired ovens. With a very fast cooking time and using minimal amounts of oil, the ingredients maintained their freshness, vitamin counts remained high and the fat content stayed low. The gourmet pizza was born!

This new style of pizza received favourable reaction from all types of pizza connoisseurs: the young, the middle-aged and the elderly. Indeed, the gourmet pizza stretches across the generation gap and, with its mass market appeal, will remain as one of the staple foods within our society. So long as there are people willing to create and sample new produce, or reinvent the old, the pizza will retain its popularity.

# The Basics

## THE BASIC EQUIPMENT

### STONEWARE

At the restaurant, we use specially imported pizza ovens to achieve a crisp, golden pizza base. These ovens run at a much higher temperature than your average domestic oven. The best way to achieve a similar result at home is to cook your pizza on an unglazed terracotta tile.

A hand-moulded tile about 32 cm (12 in.) square and approximately 2 cm (¾ in.) thick is ideal. These moulded tiles retain the heat better than factory-extruded ones. They are fairly inexpensive and are available from terracotta studios or tiling stores.

### METALWARE

**PIZZA PADDLE:** An extremely handy piece of equipment, a pizza paddle or baker's peel is basically an oversized egg slice. It is about 26 cm x 26 cm (10 in. x 10 in.), with a bevelled edge to allow you to slip the paddle under your pizza and lift it into the oven with no mess or fuss, and, most importantly, in one piece! A gentle push and the pizza slides off onto the cooking tile.

When the pizza is done, the paddle will easily slide under it and retrieve it from the stoneware on which it was baked. Alternatively, a pair of wide spatulas will do the job, but not as safely as a paddle.

**PIZZA CUTTER:** I highly recommend using a pizza cutter or wheel to slice your pizza, but don't try and race through the pizza as you may end up with a big mess and all the topping dragged from one side to the other. With some of the dessert pizzas that appear later in the book, it is safest to cut them with a large chopping or cook's knife. This helps to keep the ingredients in place and makes the presentation a lot better.

**FOOD PROCESSOR OR MIXER:** There are number of good food processors on the market, so shop around for one that will easily accommodate a batch of pizza dough. If you don't have a food processor, there is no need to worry as I have included a method using the good, old-fashioned rolling pin; it will just take a little bit longer and require a little more effort.

### HARDWARE

**SCALES:** Scales are a necessary tool for any successful baking. It is essential that they are accurate, especially when dealing with yeast.

## GENERAL

The following general equipment will also be needed when making your pizzas:

- a good selection of mixing bowls
- a large wire whisk
- a measuring jug or cup
- a chopping board
- saucepans
- a frying pan or skillet
- roasting trays

# THE BASIC INGREDIENTS

~~~

## FLOUR

Basically, three varieties of flour are used throughout this book. All are readily available from your supermarket.

PLAIN OR ALL-PURPOSE FLOUR: This flour is of medium protein or gluten content. Gluten is what gives flour its strength and structure when used in dough products. Any commercially available plain flour is suitable.

WHOLEMEAL OR WHOLE-WHEAT FLOUR: Unlike plain or all-purpose flour, this flour still contains the wheat germ. This means it is higher in fibre and nutrition. Use one of the brands readily available from your supermarket.

SEMOLINA: This flour is made from crushing a cereal, usually hard wheat,

into granules. Semolina that has been medium to finely ground is required. Once your pizza dough has been rolled out to shape, the board is sprinkled with semolina and the dough placed on top. This stops the pizza base from sticking to the board and, when you are ready to place it into the oven, it will slide off easily. You will not need a great deal of this flour. It lasts indefinitely, so simply buy a packet and store in an airtight container until needed.

## YEAST

Yeast is a minute form of plant life that belongs to the fungi family and can multiply rapidly under ideal conditions.

ACTIVE DRY YEAST: A high-activity yeast that is dried and vacuum-packed to preserve its freshness and life. It is conveniently packaged in sachet form and will remain active for at least two years. This is the yeast with which we will be dealing. It is readily available from your supermarket.

COMPRESSED FRESH YEAST: The fresh or compressed yeast that is sold in larger quantities reacts more quickly in doughmaking, but it has a short shelf life and is generally available only to commercial kitchens.

## OLIVE OIL

The secret to producing the desired crispy crust for your pizza lies in the oil content of your dough: the oil provides an improved heat transfer between the crust and the baking surface, as well as imparting wonderful flavour to the dough.

**POMACE**: This is essentially the second grade of olive oil. It has a mild olive taste and is fairly cheap to use, but it may have a cloudy look to it.

**VIRGIN**: This is the among the top lines of olive oil. As its name suggests, it comes from the first pressing of the olive and is stronger in taste and flavour than pomace. Virgin olive oil is topped in quality only by extra virgin olive oil, which also comes from the first pressing of the olives.

## TOMATO SAUCE

The tomato or pizza sauce that makes up the base of your pizza topping requires a few simple considerations to be taken into account: how sweet it should be, how herbaceous and what consistency to make it. It took eight months of testing and development to arrive at the tomato sauce we use at the Red Centre restaurant, and this recipe is given later on in the book.

In season, fresh tomatoes are wonderful to use in your base sauce. However, you will have to allow for changes in the water content of the fruit — your sauce may be too thin at some times and too thick at others. Canned crushed tomatoes are always the same consistency so they make an excellent choice for your base sauce.

## CHEESE

Since the introduction of the gourmet pizza, gone are the days when the only cheese you would find on a pizza was mozzarella. At the Red Centre we use a range of eight to ten different cheeses.

Below is an outline of the styles and characteristics of some of these.

**MOZZARELLA**: The godfather of pizza cheeses, mozzarella originated in southern Italy. It has a mild flavour and a soft, white texture, with good melting properties.

**BLUE CHEESE**: Choose a young, firm blue cheese with a sharp flavour, such as young Gorgonzola or the Australian blue cheese, Great Southern Blue. Once matured, the cheese becomes much smoother, but with a bolder blue flavour.

**GOAT CHEESE OR CHÈVRE**: This is a very creamy and flavoursome cheese with acidic properties. Each brand of goat cheese will vary in taste, so it's important that you try them and select the one you prefer. Types to choose from include Montrachet, Bucheron and Milawa.

**BRIE**: Choose a rich, full-cream Brie with a sweet aftertaste, such as the French *Brie de Meaux* or the Australian Southcape Brie or Cape Wickham Brie. These last two cheeses are classified as white mould cheeses. They are surface-ripened using white penicillin mould that changes the curd and flavour. The ripening process starts from the surface and progresses to the centre as the cheese matures.

**BOCCONCINI**: A soft curd cheese of a mozzarella type, bocconcini is a very mild cheese, slightly acidic in flavour.

**GRANA PADANO PARMESAN**: This is a grainy or granulated Parmesan, intense and sharp in taste, and is aged between 14 and 18 months before being sold. It is produced in Italy. About one-quarter of Italian cow's milk production is taken up in the manufacture of grana cheeses.

**CHEDDAR**: At the restaurant, we use Stokes Point Cheddar, a young, pleasantly smooth-flavoured cheese with a lingering full flavour, an open texture and a crumbly consistency. There is a large range of cheddar cheeses to choose from, so shop around until you find the one that you prefer.

## SMALLGOODS

In this section I am simply providing my preferred choice for smallgoods. They are produced by Tibaldi, but there will be equivalents at your supermarket or delicatessen. The strength and flavour will vary from brand to brand, so once again shop around until you find the brand that you prefer.

**PEPERONI**: This Italian salami is a pork and beef mixture that is finely minced or ground. Peperoni is spicy and hot, with a slightly smoky flavour.

**SICILIANO**: A traditional coarse, chunky salami, Siciliano is highly flavoured with more than a liberal sprinkling of crushed chilli peppers and sweet tomato paste. This salami is very hot!

**PROSCIUTTO PARMA**: Whole pork legs are trimmed and aged with sea salt, then massaged by hand to expel excess moisture and aged with the bone in for 12 months to develop flavour and taste. The final product is sensational cured meat that is full of flavour, providing an excellent accompaniment to many dishes.

## SEAFOOD

There are only two rules to apply to any seafood that you use: always buy the best and make sure it is fresh. When precooking seafood, be sure to cook the item until it is 'just done', that is, so that the seafood is almost cooked, but not quite. Bear in mind that the pizza will be going back into the oven to cook and so will any seafood that is topping it.

The time to go to the market to buy your produce is after you have decided to make a seafood pizza. You may, in fact, see other shellfish there that you would like to try, such as yabbies, crayfish, bug meat or slipper lobsters, to name but a few.

**PRAWNS OR SHRIMP**: Frozen prawns (shrimp) are acceptable for use on pizza toppings, but it is far better to go to the trouble of buying fresh ones. Always peel and devein them before use.

**SCALLOPS**: Buy fresh scallops from your local fishmonger or go to the markets to select them. You may choose to buy your scallops complete with roe to add extra flavour or, alternatively, simply use the scallop without roe.

**OCTOPUS**: A wonderful and interesting item to put on your pizzas, but be sure to clean the octopus properly and take care not to overcook. Select baby octopus as it looks better on the finished pizza and will not have to be trimmed as much.

**MUSSELS**: If the prospect of steaming open your own mussels seems a bit daunting, buy mussels that have been marinated in brine instead.

OYSTERS: Choose fresh oysters in the half shell so that you get the real flavour without the addition of salty brine. These delicate bivalves deserve to be served *au naturel*.

SMOKED SALMON: You may find salmon pieces or trimmings at the markets, which are perfect for using on a pizza. Otherwise, use sliced smoked salmon. It may be quite expensive, but you will only need about 100 g (3 oz) per pizza.

CAVIAR: For some people, the thought of caviar on a pizza may well be hard to imagine, but it is delicious when nestled on a large dollop of crème fraîche on top of smoked salmon. There is also some very good salmon roe available that is good to use. Although it is orange in colour and larger in roe size than caviar, it provides an equally acceptable topping.

From time to time I use other seasonal seafood such as tuna, sardines, scampi, marron and Atlantic salmon as pizza toppings. You are really only limited by your imagination when it comes to making your own creations. Don't be afraid to experiment with new things.

## WHAT'S INSTANTLY AVAILABLE?

PIZZA BASES: Much to my surprise, I was delighted to find a wide range of pizza bases for sale. They vary in size from small (about 16 cm (6 in.) in diameter) through to large (about 26 cm (10 in.)). These bases are available fresh, vacuum-sealed or frozen, so you can always have some in the freezer for the times when you crave a pizza, but don't have time to make the dough.

Another alternative is to use pocket or pita breads, which make a suitable base and are available in reduced salt, yeast-free, wholemeal (whole-wheat) and regular forms. It is really a matter of choice and finding out what you like, as some bases may be too thick, too dry or just not quite right from some reason.

TOMATO SAUCE BASE: I have found two products on the supermarket shelves that are called 'pizza sauce'. These can provide a quick, tasty base sauce when you don't have enough time to make your own. You may also like to try some of the chunky-style pasta sauces that are commercially available.

PIZZA CHEESES: Mozzarella is one cheese that is abundantly available, whether it be grated or in the traditional small balls. Most of the cheeses I have already mentioned are on hand in the cheese section of good supermarkets or at delicatessens, but feel free to replace them with other favourites or to try some new ones.

## THE PANTRY

Following is a collection of the base recipes that are used several times throughout this book. They should be made ahead of time, so you may need to plan ahead before diving in to make your first pizza. All sauces will last in the refrigerator for up to two weeks, some even longer, so you can keep any leftovers for your next pizza session.

# BASIC PIZZA DOUGH

〜〜〜

This recipe makes eight dough balls. Any excess dough can be stored in the freezer until required.

## STARTER

3 scant tablespoons (20 g, ¾ oz) active dry yeast

5 teaspoons caster (superfine) sugar

⅔ cup (150 mL, 5 fl oz) lukewarm or room-temperature water (the water temperature should not exceed 37°C (98°F))

2 cups (250 g, 8 oz) plain (all-purpose) flour

## DOUGH

¼ cup (65 mL, 2 fl oz) olive oil

1¾ cups (440 mL, 14 fl oz) lukewarm or room-temperature water

2 teaspoons salt

6 cups (750 g, 1½ lb) plain (all-purpose) flour

MAKES 8 DOUGH BALLS

## STARTER

Combine the yeast and sugar with the water in a small bowl. Whisk together to incorporate. Pour into the mixing bowl of a food processor. Add the flour and pulse (using an on/off action) to mix.

## DOUGH

Pour the olive oil into the water. Mix the salt into the flour and add to the starter dough in the food processor (fitted with a metal blade). Add the oil/water mixture. Pulse until a ball starts to form, 1–2 minutes should be sufficient. You should now have a nice, smooth dough.

Remove the dough from the processor and dust lightly with flour to absorb any excess moisture. Place in a lightly floured bowl and cover with a damp cloth. Leave to rise or prove in a warm place until the dough has doubled in size, about 30 minutes. If you are not going to use the dough immediately, place in the refrigerator. This will slow down the proving process and prevent the dough from growing too much in size.

Knock back (punch down) the dough. This process is where the dough is smacked to release any gases that may have built up during proving. Roll the dough back into a ball and divide into 8 pieces (about 250 g (8 oz) each). Roll each piece into a ball, then wrap each one in plastic wrap (cling film) and return to the refrigerator until you are ready to use for the pizza base. If you are not going to use the dough immediately, store in the freezer until needed.

When you want to make your pizza, remove the dough ball from the refrigerator and allow to stand until it reaches room temperature. This will make the dough easier to stretch and roll out.

# WHOLEMEAL PIZZA DOUGH

~~~

Although this is a wholemeal (whole-wheat) dough recipe, only a third of the flour is wholemeal flour because the plain (all-purpose) flour makes the dough lighter and easier to handle.

## STARTER

3 scant tablespoons (20 g, ¾ oz) active dry yeast
5 teaspoons caster (superfine) sugar
⅔ cup (150 mL, 5 fl oz) lukewarm or room-temperature water (the water temperature should not exceed 37°C (98°F))
2 cups (250 g, 8 oz) plain (all-purpose) flour

## DOUGH

¼ cup (65 mL, 2 fl oz) olive oil
1¾ cups (440 mL, 14 fl oz) lukewarm or room-temperature water
2 teaspoons salt
4 cups (500 g, 1 lb) plain (all-purpose) flour
2 cups (250 g, 8 oz) wholemeal (whole-wheat) flour

MAKES 8 DOUGH BALLS

The method for wholemeal pizza dough is the same as for the basic dough (see opposite).

## TO MAKE THE DOUGH BY HAND

Combine the dry ingredients in a large bowl and make a well in the centre. Pour the liquid ingredients in the well and gradually incorporate the dry ingredients from around the sides of the bowl. Once the ingredients are combined, remove from the bowl and knead the dough vigorously on a floured bench for 5–10 minutes or until the dough is smooth.

Transfer to a large bowl lightly dusted with flour and cover with a damp cloth. Leave the dough to rise or prove in a warm place until it has doubled in size, about 30 minutes. Once again, if you are not going to use the dough straight away, place it in the refrigerator and allow to prove over several hours instead. Continue as for processor dough (see opposite).

# HOW TO ROLL YOUR DOUGH

Clear some space on your work bench or counter. You will remember that I spoke about semolina earlier in this chapter; well, this is where you use it. Lightly sprinkle both the bench and your dough ball with semolina. Take the dough ball and flatten it out using the palms of your hands, then place it on the bench to begin rolling.

Start gently working the dough with a rolling pin. Give it several rolls back and forth to make it egg-shaped as you face it, and then turn it around 90 degrees, so that the egg shape is horizontal to you. Sprinkle some more semolina over the dough if it is starting to stick. Continue rolling the dough in each direction until it becomes round and approximately 26 cm (10 in.) in diameter, or the size of a medium pizza.

Take a flat tray with no edges (such as a baking sheet) and sprinkle it liberally with semolina. This is what you will make your pizza on. Place the pizza base onto the tray and let the dough relax or rest for 5 minutes. (This is the ideal time to roll out another base.) You are now ready to top your pizza.

# PIZZA SAUCE
~~~

The quantities below will make enough tomato sauce for approximately six pizzas.

2 teaspoons olive oil
150 g (5 oz) onions, diced
1 teaspoon crushed garlic
8 basil leaves, freshly chopped
1 tablespoon tomato paste (purée)
1⅔ cups (425 g, 14 oz) crushed tomatoes

MAKES APPROXIMATELY 2 CUPS
(500 ML, 16 FL OZ)

Heat the olive oil in a medium saucepan over a medium heat. Add the onion and garlic. Sauté for 3–5 minutes until the onion is transparent. Add the remaining ingredients and bring to the boil. Remove from the heat and blend or process the mixture into a purée. Allow to cool. Store in an airtight container in the refrigerator until ready to use.

OPPOSITE: *Cherry Tomato, Ricotta, Roast Garlic and Pesto*

# PESTO SAUCE

〰️

A thick, fragrant sauce made from olive oil, basil and garlic which has a multitude of uses, its robust flavour enhances and complements many a pizza at our restaurant. This pesto will last indefinitely if stored in the refrigerator, so make a batch and you'll have it on hand whenever the urge strikes you. This pesto is cooked and will therefore last longer than uncooked varieties, especially as it does not contain Parmesan cheese.

1 cup (250 mL, 8 fl oz) olive oil
1 large brown (yellow) onion, diced
⅓ cup (60 g, 2 oz) pine nuts
8 cloves garlic, crushed
3 large handfuls of fresh basil leaves
salt and freshly ground black pepper,
    to taste

MAKES APPROXIMATELY 2 CUPS
(500 ML, 16 FL OZ)

Heat half of the olive oil in a medium saucepan over a medium heat. Add the onion, pine nuts and garlic. Cook, stirring continuously, until the pine nuts start to turn golden (be careful, as they will quickly scorch). Add the basil and the remainder of the oil. Simmer the mixture for 3–5 minutes, then remove from the heat.

Place the mixture in an electric blender or food processor. Blend or process until smooth, then season with salt and pepper. Store in an airtight container in the refrigerator until ready to use.

# BARBECUE SAUCE

〰️

If you feel up to making your own barbecue sauce, here's a recipe for one. It can be used as the base sauce when making your pizzas.

1 tablespoon olive oil
2 medium Spanish (red) onions, diced
1 teaspoon crushed garlic
1⅔ cups (400 mL, 13 fl oz) tomato sauce
    (ketchup)
⅓ cup (90 mL, 3 fl oz) Worcestershire
    sauce
1½ tablespoons cider vinegar
1 teaspoon Dijon mustard
2 tablespoons (soft) brown sugar
1 tablespoon chilli powder
1 tablespoon paprika
¼ teaspoon cayenne or red pepper
¼ teaspoon ground coriander
¼ teaspoon ground cumin
1 teaspoon liquid smoke (available from
    good delicatessens or Tex Mex supply
    stores)

MAKES APPROXIMATELY 3 CUPS
(750 ML, 24 FL OZ)

Heat the olive oil in a saucepan over a medium heat. Add the onion and garlic; sauté until they are transparent. Add the remaining ingredients and reduce the heat to low. Simmer uncovered for 15 minutes, stirring occasionally. Store the sauce in an airtight container in the refrigerator until ready to use.

OPPOSITE: *Barbecue Prawn with Brie and Coriander*

# ROAST VEGETABLES

~~~

The most common roast vegetables used in the creation of our pizzas include tomatoes, capsicum (sweet or bell peppers) and onions. Here are basic methods for preparing each item.

## ROAST TOMATOES

Use the small- to medium-size Roma or egg (plum) tomatoes. To prepare for roasting, simply cut in half lengthways and lay face up on a roasting pan. Season with salt and freshly ground black pepper. Bake in a cool oven at 140°C (275°F/gas mark 1) for 30–40 minutes or until the tomatoes appear dried out and reduced in size.

What you are doing here is removing the water from within the tomatoes and concentrating the juice, making it tastier and sweeter. If you wish, you can take the drying process further and completely dry out the tomatoes to make your own 'oven-dried' tomatoes. These can be stored in jars in canola or olive oil.

For a typical pizza, you will need about 4–6 whole tomatoes.

## ROAST ONIONS

The purple Spanish onions are best for this as they add a wonderful colour to the pizza, along with a much milder taste than brown (yellow) or white onions. Size isn't important when selecting your onions as they are cut into wedges before roasting.

Prepare three to four onions at a time. Peel the onions and cut lengthways into wedges no wider than 3 cm (1 in.). Place in a roasting pan with a little olive or vegetable oil. Season with salt and freshly ground black pepper.

Roast at 170°C (325°F/gas mark 3) for 10 minutes. Stir the onions and place back in the oven for another 10 minutes. Remove from the oven and allow to cool. Drain any water off the onions and set them aside until ready to use. If they are going into the refrigerator, cover them with plastic wrap (cling film) or store in an airtight container.

## ROAST CAPSICUM

Roasting this vegetable develops the inbred sweetness of capsicum (sweet or bell pepper). Once roasted, peeled and cleaned, the capsicum is easily cut into a diverse range of shapes to garnish the top of your pizza.

To roast capsicums, place them on a roasting tray in the oven at 240°C (475°C/gas mark 9). Roast until their skins are evenly blistered and browned, about 20 minutes, turning them two or three times during cooking to colour evenly.

Remove from the oven and place into a metal bowl. Cover the bowl with plastic wrap (cling film). The heat from the capsicum will create steam and this will help to loosen the charred skin.

When cool enough to handle, simply pull the stems out of the capsicum and wash the skin off under cold, running water. Remove any seeds or membrane, and cut the flesh into strips or diamonds or triangles, or whatever shape takes your fancy.

## ROAST GARLIC

To do this successfully, it is better to roast several heads of garlic at the same time. The resulting garlic purée will keep for some time in an airtight container in the refrigerator.

As the garlic roasts, its pungent acids are lost and the natural sugars in it begin to caramelise, so the garlic becomes sweeter and it loses that sometimes offensive aftertaste.

Place several heads of garlic in a small roasting pan and coat with oil. Roast in the oven at 150°C (300°F/gas mark 2) for 1–2 hours or until the garlic is soft and mushy. Remove from the oven and allow to cool.

Drain off any oil and set aside. Cut the roots off the garlic and squeeze the pulp into a bowl. Discard the garlic 'shell'. Add the reserved oil to the pulp and combine thoroughly. The garlic purée is now ready to use.

# SOME IMPORTANT COOKING TIPS

The following tips are most important for the successful baking of your pizzas. If you keep them in mind every time you bake a gourmet pizza, or any pizza for that matter, you should not go far wrong.

- When topping your pizza base, always keep a 3 cm (1¼ in.) border around the edge of the base clean. Not only will your pizza look better when cooked, this also means that the topping will not ooze over the edges and stick to your pizza stone or tile.
- Always heat your pizza stones or tiles as you preheat the oven, i.e. before you put the pizza in to bake on them. This means the dough will be crisp and golden when baked, rather than soggy.
- Experiment with your oven temperature until you find the right setting. When cooking your first pizza, preheat the oven to the highest temperature setting possible (260°F/500°F/gas mark 10). It may be a good idea to turn the temperature down slightly when you put the pizza in to bake. Once you have cooked a few pizzas, you will be able to gauge exactly how hot your pizza stones or tiles become, and adjust your oven temperature accordingly.
- Use a pizza paddle or a wide spatula to place your pizza in the oven. This way the pizza can be gently slid onto the stone or tile, and you are less likely to upset the topping.
- The pizza base may puff up during cooking. If it does, simply prick the bubbles with a fork.
- When removing the pizza from the oven, you may find it easier to slide the pizza out onto a flat tray and then transfer it to a board for cutting. This will help to prevent cracking of the crust and any possible mishaps before you actually get your pizza to the table.

# OVEN TEMPERATURES AND GAS MARKS

| CELSIUS | FAHRENHEIT | GAS MARK | HEAT |
|---------|------------|----------|------|
| 110°C | 225°F | ¼ (S) | VERY COOL |
| 120°C | 250°F | ½ (S) | VERY COOL |
| 140°C | 275°F | 1 | COOL |
| 150°C | 300°F | 2 | COOL |
| 160°C | 325°F | 3 | MODERATE |
| 180°C | 350°F | 4 | MODERATE |
| 190°C | 375°F | 5 | FAIRLY HOT |
| 200°C | 400°F | 6 | FAIRLY HOT |
| 220°C | 425°F | 7 | HOT |
| 230°C | 450°F | 8 | VERY HOT |
| 240°C | 475°F | 9 | VERY HOT |
| 250°C | 500°F | 10 | VERY VERY HOT |

# POULTRY
## with a Difference

WHETHER IT'S TURKEY, DUCK OR SIMPLY CHICKEN,
THE SAME BASIC RULES APPLY.

THE BREAST FILLETS WILL ALWAYS YIELD THE
A-GRADE MEAT, BUT THEY WON'T NECESSARILY HAVE
THE BEST FLAVOUR. THE THIGH AND DRUMSTICK
(OR MARYLAND, AS IT'S SOMETIMES CALLED) IS
USUALLY A DARKER COLOURED, MORE FLAVOURSOME
CUT. IT REQUIRES SOME SKILL TO REMOVE THE
BONES, SO ASK YOUR BUTCHER OR POULTRY
SUPPLIER TO DO THIS FOR YOU IF YOU CAN'T FIND
THIGHS ALREADY BONED AT YOUR SUPERMARKET.

ALWAYS METICULOUSLY REMOVE ANY SINEW, SKIN
OR FAT FROM THE POULTRY BEFORE USING IT. WHEN
MARINATING POULTRY, A FEW INCISIONS CUT INTO
THE MEAT WILL ALLOW THE MARINADE TO BE
ABSORBED MORE QUICKLY.

FINALLY, NEVER OVERCOOK POULTRY AS IT WILL
BECOME DRY AND STRINGY.

# Tandoori Chicken

~~~

THIS PIZZA REQUIRES A FAIR BIT OF GROUNDWORK BEFORE IT CAN BE MADE,
BUT THE RESULTS ARE WELL WORTH THE PREPARATION TIME INVOLVED.
IT IS GARNISHED WITH MANGO RELISH AND CUCUMBER YOGHURT. IF ANY
RELISH OR YOGHURT IS LEFT OVER, THEY ALSO MAKE EXCELLENT
DIPS OR GARNISHES FOR COLD CUTS.

## CUCUMBER YOGHURT

½ telegraph cucumber, peeled, seeded and diced
1 tablespoon chopped fresh dill
1 tablespoon chopped fresh mint
1 cup (250 mL, 8 fl oz) plain yoghurt
salt and freshly ground black pepper, to taste

## MANGO RELISH

1 tablespoon olive oil
1 medium onion, finely diced
scant ½ cup (100 mL, 3 fl oz) cider vinegar
¼ cup (60 g, 2 oz) caster (superfine) sugar
400 g (13 oz) mango, roughly chopped
1 cup (100 g, 3 oz) dried apple
1 scant tablespoon sultanas (golden raisins)
1 scant tablespoon currants

## TANDOORI PIZZA

1 tablespoon commercially-prepared tandoori paste (such as Sharwoods)
scant ½ cup (100 mL, 3 fl oz) plain yoghurt
400 g (13 oz) chicken breasts, trimmed of any fat and sinew

salt and freshly ground black pepper, to taste
2 x 250 g (8 oz) dough balls (see page 14)
⅔ cup (150 mL, 5 fl oz) Pizza Sauce (see page 16)
1¼ cups (150 g, 5 oz) grated mozzarella cheese
⅓ cup (60 g, 2 oz) raw cashews, roughly chopped
½ small Spanish (red) onion, sliced and separated into rings
freshly cracked black pepper (optional)
chives, chopped (optional)

MAKES 2 MEDIUM PIZZAS

## CUCUMBER YOGHURT

Place the cucumber in a bowl and add the remaining ingredients. Mix well and season with salt and pepper. Set aside until ready to use. (Any leftover garnish can be stored in an airtight container in the refrigerator.)

## MANGO RELISH

Heat the olive oil in a medium saucepan over a moderate heat. Add the onion and sauté for 3 minutes or until the onion becomes transparent. Add the cider vinegar, sugar and half of the mango pulp. Cook gently until the liquid has reduced in volume by half. Add the dried apple, sultanas and currants. Bring to the boil once again and simmer gently until the mixture has thickened, about 5 minutes. Remove from the heat and set aside until ready to use.

This relish can be made when mangoes are in season and will keep in the refrigerator indefinitely. This means you can make several batches when mangoes are at their cheapest and store the relish until needed. Frozen or canned mango slices are also suitable.

## TANDOORI PIZZA

Whisk the tandoori paste and yoghurt together until the mixture is smooth and free of lumps. Place the chicken breasts in a bowl and add enough of the tandoori sauce to coat the chicken. Leave to marinate in the refrigerator for several hours or overnight.

Preheat the oven to 180°C (350°F/ gas mark 4). Place the marinated chicken on a lightly oiled baking sheet. Bake in the oven for 15 minutes or until cooked.

Allow the chicken to cool completely before cutting across the breast into very thin slices.

Place the chicken slices in a bowl and add just enough of the remaining tandoori sauce to moisten the chicken. Season with salt and pepper.

Place two pizza stones or tiles in the oven. Heat the oven to its highest possible setting (260°C/500°F/gas mark 10). Roll out the pizza dough, as described on page 16, so that you have two bases. Cover the bases with the Pizza Sauce and mozzarella cheese, keeping a 3 cm (1¼ in.) border around the edge of the dough clean.

Dot the tandoori chicken on the bases in a random pattern, leaving spaces for the other ingredients to fall into. Sprinkle with the cashews. Place the onion rings all over the top.

Using a wide spatula or pizza paddle, gently slide each pizza onto a stone or tile. Cook for 10 minutes. Remove the pizzas from the oven when cooked and golden. Season with the black pepper and garnish with some chives (if using). Slice each pizza into eight pieces and serve immediately, accompanied by the Cucumber Yoghurt and Mango Relish.

# Balmy Chicken with Pawpaw & Mango Salsa

ACCOMPANIED BY A FRAGRANT AND TASTY SALSA, THIS PIZZA
IS A TROPICAL BLEND COUPLED WITH SPRING ONIONS (SCALLIONS),
SMOKED CHICKEN AND BROCCOLI.

2 x 250 g (8 oz) dough balls
(see page 14)
150 mL (5 fl oz) Pizza Sauce
(see page 16)
1¼ cups (150 g, 5 oz) grated mozzarella
cheese
350 g (11 oz) smoked chicken, shredded
3 spring onions (scallions), sliced on the
angle, Chinese style
150 g (5 oz) bocconcini cheese, diced
2 heads of broccoli, cut into florets
and blanched until almost cooked
(about 3 minutes)

**PAWPAW AND MANGO SALSA**
1 pawpaw (papaya), peeled and diced
1 mango, peeled and diced
½ Spanish (red) onion, peeled and diced
½ lime, peeled, segmented and diced
¼ bunch of coriander (cilantro), finely
chopped
¼ teaspoon chilli paste, or to taste

MAKES 2 MEDIUM PIZZAS

Place two pizza stones or tiles in the oven. Heat the oven to its highest possible setting (260°C/500°F/gas mark 10). Roll out the pizza dough, as described on page 16, so that you have two bases. Cover the bases with the Pizza Sauce and mozzarella cheese, keeping a 3 cm (1¼ in.) border around the edge of the dough clean.

Place the smoked chicken in a random pattern on the bases, leaving spaces for other ingredients to fall into. Add the spring onion and bocconcini cheese. Top with the broccoli.

Using a wide spatula or pizza paddle, gently slide each pizza onto a stone or tile. Cook for 10 minutes. Remove the pizzas from the oven when cooked and golden. Slice each pizza into eight pieces and serve immediately, accompanied by the Pawpaw and Mango Salsa.

**PAWPAW AND MANGO SALSA**
Combine the ingredients for the salsa in a bowl. Vary the amount of chilli paste to suit your taste.

# Barbecue Chicken with Sour Cream

~~~~~~

USE OUR BARBECUE SAUCE RECIPE TO BREATHE A LITTLE 'FIRE' INTO THIS RECIPE. IT'S MAGNIFICENT WITH A LARGE DOLLOP OF SOUR CREAM HEAPED ON TOP — DEFINITELY A CROWD PLEASER.

400 g (13 oz) chicken breasts, trimmed of any fat and sinew

a little olive oil

2 cloves garlic, crushed (optional)

2 x 250 g (8 oz) dough balls (see page 14)

scant ½ cup (100 mL, 3 fl oz) Pizza Sauce (see page 16)

¼ cup (60 mL, 2 fl oz) Barbecue Sauce (see page 19)

1¼ cups (150 g, 5 oz) grated mozzarella cheese

1 avocado, peeled and cut into pieces

½ punnet (125 g, 4 oz) cherry tomatoes, halved

150 g (5 oz) Swiss cheese, cut into chunks

scant ½ cup (100 mL, 3 fl oz) sour cream

MAKES 2 MEDIUM PIZZAS

Put the chicken breasts in a bowl. Marinate with a little olive oil and the garlic (if using). Char-grill or barbecue the breasts until cooked on both sides. Allow to cool and then slice across the breasts into very thin pieces.

Meanwhile, place two pizza stones or tiles in the oven. Heat the oven to its highest possible setting (260°C/500°F/ gas mark 10). Roll out the pizza dough, as described on page 16, so that you have two bases. Cover the bases with the Pizza Sauce and mozzarella cheese, keeping a 3 cm (1¼ in.) border around the edge of the dough clean.

Place the sliced chicken in a random pattern on the bases, leaving spaces for the other ingredients to fall into. Add the avocado, cherry tomatoes and Swiss cheese.

Using a wide spatula or pizza paddle, gently slide each pizza onto a stone or tile. Cook for 10 minutes. Remove the pizzas from the oven when cooked and golden. Slice each pizza into eight pieces and serve immediately, garnished with the sour cream.

# Smoked Turkey with Black Bean & Lime Salsa

~~~

A VISUALLY APPEALING PIZZA, THIS IS OUR VERSION OF THE 'BLT' — BLACK BEAN, LIME AND TURKEY.

**BLACK BEAN AND LIME SALSA**

1 cob of fresh corn, husk and silk removed

60 g (2 oz) black (turtle) beans, cooked in salted water until tender

1 Spanish (red) onion, finely diced

¼ bunch of coriander (cilantro), freshly chopped

juice of 1 lime

2 x 250 g (8 oz) dough balls (see page 14)

⅔ cup (150 mL, 5 fl oz) Pizza Sauce (see page 16)

1¼ cups (150 g, 5 oz) grated mozzarella cheese

350 g (11 oz) smoked turkey, cut into pieces

2 teaspoons sliced jalapeño chilli peppers

¾ cup (100 g, 3 oz) grated provolone cheese (can be replaced with mozzarella cheese)

scant ½ cup (100 mL, 3 fl oz) sour cream (optional)

MAKES 2 MEDIUM PIZZAS

**BLACK BEAN AND LIME SALSA**

Preheat the oven to 170°C (325°F/gas mark 3). Wrap the corn cob in foil and roast for 20–30 minutes. Take out of the foil and remove the kernels from the cob with a knife. Combine the corn kernels and the remaining ingredients for the salsa in a bowl. Set aside.

Place two pizza stones or tiles in the oven. Heat the oven to its highest possible setting (260°C/500°F/gas mark 10). Roll out the pizza dough, as described on page 16, so that you have two bases. Cover the bases with the Pizza Sauce and mozzarella cheese, keeping a 3 cm (1¼ in.) border around the edge of the dough clean. Dot the smoked turkey on the bases in a random pattern. Add the jalapeños and small spoonfuls of the Black Bean and Lime Salsa. Sprinkle the provolone cheese over the top.

Using a wide spatula or pizza paddle, gently slide each pizza onto a stone or tile. Cook for 10 minutes. Remove the pizzas from the oven when cooked and golden. Slice each pizza into eight pieces and serve immediately, garnished with the sour cream (if using).

# Tahitian

~~~

THE PAIRING OF CURRY POWDER AND SHREDDED COCONUT IN THIS RECIPE
MAKES AN UNUSUAL BUT TASTY PIZZA.

2 x 250 g (8 oz) dough balls
  (see page 14)
⅔ cup (150 mL, 5 fl oz) Pizza Sauce
  (see page 16)
1¼ cups (150 g, 5 oz) grated mozzarella
  cheese
150 g (5 oz) scallops, seared
200 g (7 oz) smoked chicken, shredded
1 small onion (about 100 g (3 oz)),
  cut into wedges and roasted
  (see page 20)
1 red capsicum (bell pepper), diced
1 teaspoon curry powder
1½ tablespoons shredded (flaked)
  coconut
2 tablespoons chopped coriander
  (cilantro) leaves
freshly cracked black pepper, to taste

MAKES 2 MEDIUM PIZZAS

Place two pizza stones or tiles in the oven. Heat the oven to its highest possible setting (260°C/500°F/gas mark 10). Roll out the pizza dough, as described on page 16, so that you have two bases. Cover the bases with the Pizza Sauce and mozzarella cheese, keeping a 3 cm (1¼ in.) border around the edge of the dough clean.

Place the scallops in a clock-style pattern around the edge of each base. Now dot with the smoked chicken in a random pattern. Place the roast onion and capsicum on top. Lightly dust each pizza with the curry powder. Lastly, sprinkle with the coconut and coriander.

Using a wide spatula or pizza paddle, gently slide each pizza onto a stone or tile. Cook for 10 minutes. Remove the pizzas from the oven when cooked and golden. Slice each pizza into eight pieces and season with the cracked black pepper. Serve immediately.

# Mexican Chicken with Roast Garlic & Chillies

〜〜〜

MOLE, A COMPLEX MEXICAN SAUCE OF CHILLI PEPPERS WITH A HINT OF CHOCOLATE, MAKES THIS A TRULY SENSATIONAL TEX MEX STYLE PIZZA. ADJUST THE AMOUNT OF JALAPEÑO CHILLI PEPPERS TO SUIT YOUR TASTE.

1 tablespoon mole paste (Mexican ground spice seasoning, available from Tex Mex supply stores or gourmet stores)

scant ½ cup (100 mL, 3 fl oz) chicken stock

400 g (13 oz) chicken breasts, trimmed of any fat and sinew

2 x 250 g (8 oz) dough balls (see page 14)

⅔ cup (150 mL, 5 fl oz) Pizza Sauce (see page 16)

1¼ cups (150 g, 5 oz) grated mozzarella cheese

1 tablespoon roast garlic purée (see page 21)

1 tablespoon sliced jalapeño chilli peppers, or to taste

½ bunch of coriander (cilantro), freshly chopped

⅔ cup (150 g, 5 oz) Guacamole (see page 73)

sour cream, to garnish (optional)

MAKES 2 MEDIUM PIZZAS

Put the mole into a bowl and add enough of the stock to make a thick sauce. Add the chicken breasts to this mixture and marinate in the refrigerator for several hours (overnight is ideal). Roast the chicken in the oven at 180°C (350°F/gas mark 4) for 10–12 minutes. Allow to cool and cut across the breast into strips.

Place two pizza stones or tiles in the oven. Heat the oven to its highest possible setting (260°C/500°F/gas mark 10). Roll out the pizza dough, as described on page 16, so that you have two bases.

Cover the bases with the Pizza Sauce and mozzarella cheese, keeping a 3 cm (1¼ in.) border around the edge of the dough clean. Dot the chicken on the bases in a random pattern. Place small amounts of the roast garlic all over the bases. Add the jalapeños and sprinkle with the coriander.

Using a wide spatula or pizza paddle, gently slide each pizza onto a stone or tile. Cook for 10 minutes. Remove the pizzas from the oven when cooked and golden. Slice each pizza into eight pieces and garnish with the Guacamole and sour cream (if using). Serve immediately.

# Santa Fe Chicken

~~~

THIS IS A FAIRLY QUICK RECIPE TO THROW TOGETHER. THE FIRE
CONTENT OF JALAPEÑOS VARIES FROM ONE TO ANOTHER, SO TRY THEM
BEFORE BECOMING TOO GENEROUS. YOU WILL ONLY NEED ABOUT ONE SLICE
OF JALAPEÑO PER SLICE OF PIZZA.

2 x 250 g (8 oz) dough balls
   (see page 14)
⅔ cup (150 mL, 5 fl oz) Pizza Sauce
   (see page 16)
1¼ cups (150 g, 5 oz) grated mozzarella
   cheese
1 cup (60 g, 2 oz) sun-dried tomatoes
   (drained of oil), cut into chunks
250 g (8 oz) chicken, cooked and sliced
   (leftover roast chicken works well for
   this recipe)
1 medium avocado, peeled and cut into
   pieces (about 200 g (7 oz))
45 g (1½ oz) Brie cheese, sliced into
   strips about ½ cm (¼ in.) thick
12–16 slices jalapeño chilli pepper
½ bunch of coriander (cilantro) leaves,
   chopped

MAKES 2 MEDIUM PIZZAS

Place two pizza stones or tiles in the
oven. Heat the oven to its highest possible
setting (260°C/500°F/gas mark 10).
Roll out the pizza dough, as described
on page 16, so that you have two bases.
Cover the bases with the Pizza Sauce
and mozzarella cheese, keeping a 3 cm
(1¼ in.) border around the edge of the
dough clean.

Dot the sun-dried tomatoes on the
bases. Next add the chicken in a random
pattern, leaving spaces for the other
ingredients to fall into. Add the avocado,
Brie and jalapeños. Sprinkle with the
coriander.

Using a wide spatula or pizza paddle,
gently slide each pizza onto a stone or
tile. Cook for 10 minutes. Remove the
pizzas from the oven when cooked and
golden. Slice each pizza into eight pieces
and serve immediately.

# Smoked Chicken with Corn & Wild Rice

〜〜〜

TOPPED WITH CREAMED CORN AND WILD RICE INSTEAD OF THE USUAL TOMATO
SAUCE AND MOZZARELLA CHEESE, THIS IS A DELICIOUSLY DIFFERENT PIZZA.

1 x 440 g (14 oz) can creamed corn

1 cup (250 g, 8 oz) corn kernels

1⅔ cups (400 mL, 13 fl oz) thickened
(whipping, double) cream

a little cornflour (cornstarch)

salt and freshly ground black pepper,
to taste

2–3 tablespoons wild rice

2 x 250 g (8 oz) dough balls
(see page 14)

1 cup (60 g, 2 oz) sun-dried tomatoes
(drained of oil), chopped

350 g (11 oz) smoked chicken, bones
removed and chicken cut into slices

½ bunch of coriander (cilantro) leaves,
chopped (optional)

MAKES 2 MEDIUM PIZZAS

Place the creamed corn, corn kernels
and cream in a medium saucepan.
Heat gently, stirring constantly, until the
mixture comes to the boil. Add a little
cornflour to thicken the mixture slightly.
Remove from the heat and season with
salt and pepper. Set aside to cool.

Place two pizza stones or tiles in the
oven. Heat the oven to its highest possible
setting (260°C/500°F/gas mark 10).

Add the wild rice to a saucepan of
water (use about 4 parts water to 1 part
rice). Bring to the boil and cook for
15–20 minutes. When cooked, drain
and add to the creamed corn mixture.

Roll out the pizza dough, as described
on page 16, so that you have two bases.
Cover the bases with the creamed corn
mixture, keeping a 3 cm (1¼ in.) border
around the edge of the dough clean. Dot
the sun-dried tomato on the bases. Add
the chicken in a random pattern. Sprinkle
the coriander over the top (if using).

Using a wide spatula or pizza paddle,
gently slide each pizza onto a stone or
tile. Cook for 10 minutes. Remove the
pizzas from the oven when cooked and
golden. Slice each pizza into eight pieces
and serve immediately.

# Chicken Teriyaki

〜〜〜

YOU MAY DECIDE TO MAKE YOUR OWN TERIYAKI SAUCE FOR THIS PIZZA.
IF SO, THERE IS A RECIPE GIVEN FOR THIS UNDER THE ORIENTAL DUCK RECIPE.
IF NOT, SIMPLY USE A SUPERMARKET BRAND.

400 g (13 oz) chicken breasts, trimmed
  of any fat and sinew

½ cup (125 mL, 4 fl oz) teriyaki sauce
  (see page 37)

2 x 250 g (8 oz) dough balls
  (see page 14)

⅔ cup (150 mL, 5 fl oz) Pizza Sauce
  (see page 16)

1¼ cups (150 g, 5 oz) grated mozzarella
  cheese

1 medium red capsicum (bell pepper),
  diced

1 cup (60 g, 2 oz) bean sprouts

½ bunch of coriander (cilantro), freshly
  chopped

MAKES 2 MEDIUM PIZZAS

Marinate the chicken breasts in the teriyaki sauce for several hours, preferably overnight. Char-grill the marinated breasts on a barbecue or roast in the oven at 180°C (350°F/gas mark 4) until cooked. Allow to cool and then cut across the breast into slices.

Place two pizza stones or tiles in the oven. Heat the oven to its highest possible setting (260°C/500°F/gas mark 10). Roll out the pizza dough, as described on page 16, so that you have two bases. Cover the bases with the Pizza Sauce and mozzarella cheese, keeping a 3 cm (1¼ in.) border around the edge of the dough clean.

Place the chicken on the bases in a random pattern, leaving spaces for other ingredients to fall into. Add the capsicum and bean sprouts. Sprinkle with the coriander.

Using a wide spatula or pizza paddle, gently slide each pizza onto a stone or tile. Cook for 10 minutes. Remove the pizzas from the oven when cooked and golden. Slice each pizza into eight pieces and serve immediately.

# Mediterranean Chicken

WITH TASTES FROM THE SUN-DRENCHED ISLANDS OF GREECE, THIS PIZZA
USES TOMATOES, OLIVES, GARLIC AND BOCCONCINI CHEESE TO PRODUCE
A FLAVOURSOME MARRIAGE OF INGREDIENTS.

250 g (8 oz) chicken breasts, trimmed
of any fat and sinew

1½ tablespoons olive oil

2 cloves garlic, crushed

salt and freshly ground black pepper,
to taste

grated zest of 1 lemon

1½ teaspoons chopped lemon thyme
leaves

2 x 250 g (8 oz) dough balls
(see page 14)

⅔ cup (150 mL, 5 fl oz) Pizza Sauce
(see page 16)

1¼ cups (150 g, 5 oz) grated mozzarella
cheese

1 cup (60 g, 2 oz) sun-dried tomatoes
(drained of oil), roughly chopped

½ large onion (about 75 g (2½ oz)), cut
into wedges and roasted (see page 20)

60 g (2 oz) kalamata olives, pitted and
quartered

75 g (2½ oz) bocconcini cheese, cut into
1 cm (½ in.) slices

½ bunch of basil, finely sliced

MAKES 2 MEDIUM PIZZAS

Preheat the oven to 180°C (350°F/gas
mark 4). Place the chicken in a bowl.
Combine the olive oil and garlic, and rub
over the chicken. Place in a roasting pan
and cook in the oven for 12–15 minutes.
Remove the chicken from the oven, but do
not turn the oven off. When the chicken is
cool, cut it into pieces, slicing across the
breast. Place in a bowl and season with
salt and pepper. Add the lemon zest and
lemon thyme. Mix together.

Place two pizza stones or tiles in the
oven. Heat the oven to its highest possible
setting (260°C/500°F/gas mark 10). Roll
out the pizza dough, as described on
page 16, so that you have two bases.
Cover the bases with the Pizza Sauce
and mozzarella cheese, keeping a 3 cm
(1¼ in.) border around the edge of the
dough clean. Dot with the sun-dried
tomatoes first. Add the chicken pieces
in a random pattern, leaving spaces for
other ingredients to fall into. Add the
onion, olives and bocconcini cheese. Top
with the basil.

Using a wide spatula or pizza paddle,
gently slide each pizza onto a stone or
tile. Cook for 10 minutes. Remove the
pizzas from the oven when cooked and
golden. Slice each pizza into eight pieces
and serve immediately.

OPPOSITE: *Mediterranean Chicken*

# Oriental Duck

~~~

THIS PIZZA BECAME SO POPULAR THAT OUR POULTRY SUPPLIER
COULD NOT KEEP UP WITH THE DEMAND OF OUR CUSTOMERS! NOW WE
FEATURE IT FROM TIME TO TIME AS A 'PIZZA OF THE DAY' AND THE USUAL
REACTION FROM CLIENTS AND STAFF IS TO ASK WHY WE DON'T HAVE
THIS PIZZA ON THE MENU ALL THE TIME.

## TERIYAKI SAUCE

½ tablespoon sesame oil
20 g (¾ oz) fresh ginger, thinly sliced
1 onion, diced
1 teaspoon crushed garlic
2 sprigs fresh rosemary
1¼ cups (310 mL, 10 fl oz) pineapple
  juice
¾ cup (185 mL, 6 fl oz) orange juice
¼ cup (60 mL, 2 fl oz) honey
¾ cup (185 mL, 6 fl oz) soy sauce
a little cornflour (cornstarch)

## ORIENTAL DUCK

4 duck marylands (thigh and
  drumstick), trimmed of fat
⅔ cup (150 mL, 5 fl oz) Teriyaki Sauce
approx. 1 cup (250 mL, 8 fl oz) chicken
  stock (use the liquid variety if using
  instant stock)

30 g (1 oz) dried shiitake or Chinese
  mushrooms
1 tablespoon honey
2 x 250 g (8 oz) dough balls
  (see page 14)
150 mL (5 fl oz) Pizza Sauce
  (see page 16)
1¼ cups (150 g, 5 oz) grated mozzarella
  cheese
⅔ cup (45 g, 1½ oz) bean sprouts
2 small spring onions (scallions), thinly
  sliced on the angle, Chinese style
¼ cup (60 mL, 2 fl oz) Teriyaki Sauce
  (see opposite)
finely grated zest of 1 orange
sesame seeds, toasted (optional)

MAKES 2 MEDIUM PIZZAS

## TERIYAKI SAUCE

Heat the sesame oil gently over a
moderate heat in a medium saucepan.
Add the ginger, onion, garlic and
rosemary. Sauté until the onion is
transparent, then add the pineapple and
orange juices, honey and soy sauce.
Bring to the boil and thicken slightly with
a little cornflour. Set aside to cool.

OPPOSITE: *Oriental Duck*

## ORIENTAL DUCK

Preheat the oven to 150°C (300°F/ gas mark 2).

You will need to score the flesh of the duck before cooking so the marinade will penetrate through to the bone. Using a sharp knife, make several cuts across the leg, 3–4 cm (1¼–1½ in.) long. Place the duck in a shallow pan and add the Teriyaki Sauce and chicken stock. (The liquid should come halfway up the duck.)

Place the duck in the oven and cook for 1–1½ hours. When cooked, the flesh should fall off the bone easily. Remove the duck from the cooking liquid and allow to cool. Remove and discard any skin, and shred the meat from the bones. You will need 200 g (7 oz) of shredded meat for the pizza.

Reconstitute the mushrooms by placing them in a saucepan and covering with water. Add the honey and cover the pan. Simmer gently for 30–40 minutes, until the mushrooms are soft. Remove from the heat and drain. When cool, slice into thin strips.

Place two pizza stones or tiles in the oven. Heat the oven to its highest possible setting (260°C/500°F/gas mark 10). Roll out the pizza dough, as described on page 16, so that you have two bases. Cover the bases with the Pizza Sauce and mozzarella cheese, keeping a 3 cm (1¼ in.) border around the edge of the dough clean.

Place the duck on the bases in a random pattern, leaving spaces for other ingredients to fall into. Add the bean sprouts, spring onions and mushrooms. Drizzle some of the remaining Teriyaki Sauce over the top, remembering to keep the edges of the pizzas clean. Be conservative when applying this sauce as it is fairly strong. Finally, sprinkle the orange zest over the top.

Using a wide spatula or pizza paddle, gently slide each pizza onto a stone or tile. Cook for 10 minutes. Remove the pizzas from the oven when cooked and golden. Sprinkle some sesame seeds over the pizzas as a garnish (if using). Slice each pizza into eight pieces and serve immediately.

# Wild Mushroom, Chicken, Pine Nuts & Thyme

~~~

AN EARTHY, RUSTIC PIZZA COMBINING BASIC FLAVOURS THAT COMPLEMENT
EACH OTHER WELL. THE THYME CAN BE REPLACED WITH LEMON THYME TO ADD
ANOTHER DIMENSION IN TASTE AND FRAGRANCE.

2 x 250 g (8 oz) dough balls
(see page 14)
⅔ cup (150 mL, 5 fl oz) Pizza Sauce
(see page 16)
1¼ cups (150 g, 5 oz) grated mozzarella
cheese
a little olive oil
750 g (1½ lb) field or oyster or shimeji
mushrooms, cut into ½ cm (¼ in.)
slices
¼ bunch of thyme, stems discarded and
leaves and chopped
salt and freshly ground black pepper,
to taste
400 g (13 oz) chicken breasts, trimmed
of any fat and sinew, roasted and
sliced
6 spring onions (scallions), sliced on the
angle, Chinese style
¼ cup (45 g, 1½ oz) pine nuts, toasted

MAKES 2 MEDIUM PIZZAS

Place two pizza stones or tiles in the
oven. Heat the oven to its highest possible
setting (260°C/500°F/gas mark 10).
Roll out the pizza dough, as described on
page 16, so that you have two bases.
Cover the bases with the Pizza Sauce
and mozzarella cheese, keeping a 3 cm
(1¼ in.) border around the edge of the
dough clean.

Heat the olive oil in a pan until quite
hot. Add the mushrooms and sauté for
2–3 minutes. Add the thyme and season
with salt and pepper. Remove the
mushrooms from the pan and drain on
paper towels or absorbent kitchen paper.

Place the chicken on the bases in
a random pattern, leaving spaces for
other ingredients to fall into. Add the
mushrooms, spring onions and pine nuts.

Using a wide spatula or pizza paddle,
gently slide each pizza onto a stone or
tile. Cook for 10 minutes. Remove the
pizzas from the oven when cooked and
golden. Slice each pizza into eight pieces
and serve immediately.

# Thai Chicken

~~~

A RELATIVELY SIMPLE RECIPE THAT HAS GRADUALLY EVOLVED WITH EACH
NEW MENU AT THE RESTAURANT TO BECOME A BALANCE OF HOT AND TASTY. IF YOU
PREFER A MILDER FLAVOUR, SIMPLY REDUCE THE AMOUNT OF RED CURRY
PASTE USED IN THE SAUCE.

## THAI SAUCE

1 teaspoon vegetable oil
2 teaspoons red curry paste
1½ tablespoons (soft) brown sugar
1 x 400 mL (13 fl oz) can coconut milk
1 teaspoon dried lemon grass
juice and grated zest of 1 lime
1 tablespoon cornflour (cornstarch)
a little water
¾ cup (225 g, 7 oz) crunchy peanut
  butter
1 tablespoon fish sauce (nam pla)

400 g (13 oz) chicken breasts, trimmed
  of any fat and sinew
a little oil
2 x 250 g (8 oz) dough balls
  (see page 14)
1¼ cups (150 g, 5 oz) grated mozzarella
  cheese
1 medium carrot, cut into fine julienne
1 cup (60 g, 2 oz) bean sprouts
5 spring onions (scallions), sliced on the
  angle, Chinese style
½ bunch of coriander (cilantro), leaves
  picked and chopped

MAKES 2 MEDIUM PIZZAS

## THAI SAUCE

Heat the vegetable oil in a medium
saucepan over a medium heat. Add
the curry paste and stir through. Stir in
the sugar and mix well. Add the coconut
milk, lemon grass and lime juice and
zest. Bring to the boil.

Make a paste of the cornflour with a
little water. Stir into the sauce to thicken
slightly. Strain this mixture and then add
the peanut butter and the fish sauce. Set
aside to cool.

Place the chicken breasts in a bowl
or shallow dish. Add enough of the Thai
Sauce to marinate the chicken. Cover and
leave in the refrigerator overnight. (The
leftover sauce can be stored in an airtight
container in the refrigerator until needed
for the base sauce.)

Preheat the oven to 160°C (325°F/
gas mark 3). Place the chicken breasts
on a lightly oiled oven tray or baking
sheet. Roast for 12–15 minutes. Remove
the chicken from the oven and allow the
chicken to cool completely. Slice into
strips across the breast. Use some of the
Thai Sauce to moisten the chicken slightly.

Place two pizza stones or tiles in the
oven. Heat the oven to its highest possible

setting (260°C/500°F/gas mark 10).Roll out the pizza dough, as described on page 16, so that you have two bases. Cover the bases with the Thai Sauce and mozzarella cheese, keeping a 3 cm (1¼ in.) border around the edge of the dough clean.

Place the chicken on the bases in a random pattern, leaving spaces for other ingredients to fall into. Add the carrot, bean sprouts and spring onion. Sprinkle the coriander over the top.

Using a wide spatula or pizza paddle, gently slide each pizza onto a stone or tile. Cook for 10 minutes. Remove the pizzas from the oven when cooked and golden. Slice each pizza into eight pieces and serve immediately.

# Smoked Chicken, Eggplant, Roma Tomatoes, Provolone & Basil

~~~~~~

THIS PIZZA HAS ITS OWN TOMATO SAUCE BASE — ONE WITHOUT THE SPICE CONTENT OF THE REGULAR PIZZA SAUCE — TO ALLOW THE SUBTLE FLAVOURS OF THE TOPPINGS TO BE FULLY APPRECIATED. THE SMOKED CHICKEN CAN BE REPLACED WITH LEFTOVER ROAST CHICKEN OR EVEN SMOKED HAM IF YOU PREFER.

## TOMATO SAUCE

1 x 440 mL (14 fl oz) can good-quality crushed tomatoes
2 teaspoons olive oil
1 brown (yellow) onion, finely diced
1 teaspoon crushed garlic
4 basil leaves, finely sliced

2 x 250 g (8 oz) dough balls (see page 14)
⅔ cup (150 mL, 5 fl oz) tomato sauce (see above)
1¼ cups (150 g, 5 oz) grated mozzarella cheese
400 g (13 oz) smoked chicken or leftover roast chicken, shredded or sliced into pieces
1 small eggplant (aubergine), cut into slices 1 cm (½ in.) thick and roasted (see page 122)
2 small Roma (egg, plum) tomatoes, sliced into ½ cm (¼ in.) rings

125 g (4 oz) provolone cheese, cut into chunks
8 basil leaves, finely sliced
freshly cracked black pepper, to taste

MAKES 2 MEDIUM PIZZAS

## TOMATO SAUCE

Put the crushed tomatoes into a saucepan over a medium heat. Reduce the tomatoes in volume by half. Heat the olive oil in a separate pan over a medium heat. Add the onion and garlic. Sauté until transparent. Add the basil and sauté for another minute before adding the reduced tomatoes. Mix thoroughly. Remove from the heat and allow to cool.

Place two pizza stones or tiles in the oven. Heat the oven to its highest possible setting (260°C (500°F/gas mark 10). Roll out the pizza dough, as described on page 16, so that you have two bases. Cover the bases with the tomato sauce and mozzarella cheese, keeping a 3 cm (1¼ in.) border around the edge of the dough clean.

Place the smoked chicken on the bases in a random pattern, leaving spaces for other ingredients to fall into. Cut the eggplant slices into quarters and place on the bases in a random pattern. Add the tomato. Scatter the provolone cheese over the top.

Using a wide spatula or pizza paddle, gently slide each pizza onto a stone or tile. Cook for 10 minutes, Remove the pizza from the oven when cooked and golden. Slice each pizza into eight pieces and sprinkle the basil over the top. Serve immediately, garnished with the black pepper.

# Barbecued Chicken with Flat-Leaf Parsley, Barbecue Corn & Mint

~~~

THE CHICKEN IS BEST COOKED ON THE GRILL BARS OF A BARBECUE TO GIVE IT THAT DISTINCTIVE SMOKY, CHARRED FLAVOUR. THE CORN CAN BE COOKED AT THE SAME TIME.

1 tablespoon olive oil
1 teaspoon crushed garlic
2 teaspoons chopped fresh flat-leaf (Italian) parsley
2 large chicken breast fillets (tenderloin), trimmed of any fat and sinew
salt and freshly ground black pepper, to taste
2 medium corn cobs, husks and silks removed
a little butter
2 x 250 g (8 oz) dough balls (see page 14)
⅔ cup (150 mL, 5 fl oz) Pizza Sauce (see page 16)
1¼ cups (150 g, 5 oz) grated mozzarella cheese
8 mint leaves, freshly chopped
sour cream, to garnish (optional)
a little Tabasco Sauce (optional)

MAKES 2 MEDIUM PIZZAS

Put the olive oil in a small bowl. Add the garlic and parsley. Pound the chicken breasts so that they are the same thickness all over. Season with salt and pepper. Marinate the breasts in the olive oil mixture.

Bring a saucepan of salted water to the boil. Add the corn cobs. Simmer for 10–15 minutes, depending on size. Remove from the pan and drain.

Wrap each corn cob in foil with a little butter, salt and pepper. Place the foiled corn on the grill bars of your barbecue. Roast over a medium heat for 10 minutes, turning every 3 minutes or so. Remove the corn from the barbecue and open the foil.

When the corn is cool enough to handle, take a small, sharp knife and cut the kernels off the cobs. It will be easier if you slice the cob in half first and then straighten the end. This way you will be able to stand the cob on its end and slice straight down. Set the corn kernels aside.

Meanwhile, place the chicken breasts on the grill. Sear for about 2 minutes, before turning the breasts 90 degrees and cooking for another 2 minutes. This will make a criss-cross pattern on the chicken. Turn the breasts over and repeat the process. Remove from the barbecue and allow to cool. Cut into slices about ½ cm (¼ in.) thick.

Place two pizza stones or tiles in the oven. Heat the oven to its highest possible setting (260°C/500°F/gas mark 10). Roll out the pizza dough, as described on page 16, so that you have two bases. Cover the bases with the Pizza Sauce and mozzarella cheese, keeping a 3 cm (1¼ in.) border around the edge of the dough clean.

Place the chicken on the bases in a random pattern. Sprinkle generously with the corn kernels. (Some extra mozzarella cheese over the top will help hold the topping in place.)

Using a wide spatula or pizza paddle, gently slide each pizza onto a stone or tile. Cook for 10 minutes. Remove from the oven when cooked and golden. Slice each pizza into eight pieces. Sprinkle the mint over the top and season with black pepper. Garnish with a dollop of sour cream and a few splashes of Tabasco Sauce (if using). Serve immediately.

# Grilled Chicken, Goat Cheese, Roast Peppers, Pine Nuts & Raisins

~~~

THE ACIDITY OF THE GOAT CHEESE ON THIS PIZZA PROVIDES A WONDERFUL COMPLEMENT TO THE SWEETNESS OF THE ROAST PEPPERS. IT BLENDS WITH THE PINE NUTS AND RAISINS TO MAKE A LUSCIOUS, CREAMY PIZZA. BE SURE TO TOP WITH A FEW GRINDS OF FRESH BLACK PEPPER.

2 x 250 g (8 oz) dough balls
(see page 14)
⅔ cup (150 mL, 5 fl oz) Pizza Sauce
(see page 16)
1¼ cups (150 g, 5 oz) grated mozzarella
cheese
400 g (13 oz) chicken breasts, trimmed
of any fat and sinew, cooked and
sliced
100 g (3 oz) goat cheese
1 red capsicum (bell pepper), roasted
and cut into chunks (see page 20)
3 tablespoons pine nuts
2 tablespoons raisins, soaked in warm
water to soften

MAKES 2 MEDIUM PIZZAS

Place two pizza stones or tiles in the oven. Heat the oven to its highest possible setting (260°C/500°F/gas mark 10). Roll out the pizza dough, as described on page 16, so that you have two bases. Cover the bases with the Pizza Sauce and mozzarella cheese, keeping a 3 cm (1¼ in.) border around the edge of the dough clean.

Dot the chicken on the bases in a random pattern. Add the goat cheese, capsicum, pine nuts and raisins.

Using a wide spatula or pizza paddle, gently slide each pizza onto a stone or tile. Cook for 10 minutes. Remove the pizzas from the oven when cooked and golden. Slice each pizza into eight pieces and serve immediately.

# Pizza con CARNE

THE TOPPINGS IN THIS CHAPTER ENCOMPASS A WIDE RANGE OF MEATS — FROM BEEF, LAMB AND PORK, TO SALAMI, SAUSAGE AND PROSCIUTTO. ALL RECIPES ASSUME THAT ANY FAT HAS BEEN REMOVED FROM FRESH MEAT, INCLUDING SINEW AND GRISTLE.

WHEN COOKING PIECES OF MEAT FOR PIZZA TOPPINGS, WHETHER THEY BE STRIPS OR MEDALLIONS, BE SURE TO KEEP THE MEAT UNDERCOOKED OR 'PINK' IN THE MIDDLE. DON'T WORRY, AS IT WILL BE COOKED FURTHER WHEN THE PIZZA IS BAKED.

WHERE POSSIBLE, USE THE RECOMMENDED CUTS OF MEAT, AS SUBSTITUTIONS MAY NOT NECESSARILY GIVE THE SAME RESULT. IF IN DOUBT, ASK YOUR BUTCHER.

# Ham, Brie & Spinach

~~~~~~

A TYPICAL FLORENTINE BREAKFAST OR LUNCHEON SPECIAL. ALTHOUGH
BRIE CHEESE REPLACES THE TRADITIONAL EGG, THIS PIZZA STILL RETAINS THAT
SIGNATURE RICH, CREAMY FINISH. BE SURE TO FINISH WITH A FEW GRINDS
OF FRESH BLACK PEPPER.

2 x 250 g (8 oz) dough balls
   (see page 14)
⅔ cup (150 mL, 5 fl oz) Pizza Sauce
   (see page 16)
1¼ cups (150 g, 5 oz) grated mozzarella
   cheese
200 g (7 oz) sliced double-smoked ham,
   cut into quarters
1 small Spanish (red) onion (about 75 g
   (2½ oz)), cut into quarters and roasted
   (see page 20)
100 g (3 oz) Brie cheese, cut into slices
   ½ cm (¼ in.) thick
16 baby spinach leaves, stems removed
a little olive oil
½ teaspoon cumin seeds (optional)

MAKES 2 MEDIUM PIZZAS

Place two pizza stones or tiles in the
oven. Heat the oven to its highest possible
setting (260°C/500°F/gas mark 10).
Roll out the pizza dough, as described
on page 16, so that you have two bases.
Cover the bases with the Pizza Sauce
and mozzarella cheese, keeping a 3 cm
(1¼ in.) border from the edge of the
dough clean.

Place the ham on the bases in a
random pattern, leaving spaces for other
ingredients to fall into. Add the onion.
Break the slices of Brie into 3 cm (1¼ in.)
lengths and place on the pizza. Put the
spinach leaves in a bowl and drizzle
with a little olive oil. Toss the leaves
thoroughly to coat them and then place
on the pizza. Sprinkle the cumin seeds
over the top (if using).

Using a wide spatula or pizza paddle,
gently slide each pizza onto a stone or
tile. Cook for 10 minutes. Remove the
pizzas from the oven when cooked and
golden. Slice each pizza into eight pieces
and serve immediately.

# Blackbean Beef

~~~

INSPIRED BY CHINESE CUISINE, THIS PIZZA GETS ITS PRINCIPAL FLAVOUR FROM CARAMELISING THE BLACKBEAN SAUCE AROUND THE BEEF. IT CARRIES A DISTINCTIVE FLAVOUR WHICH I AM SURE YOU'VE ENCOUNTERED IN THE PAST, EVEN IF NOT NECESSARILY ON A PIZZA!

350 g (11 oz) topside or rump beef, cut into strips about 3 cm x 1 cm (1¼ in. x ½ in.)

1 tablespoon blackbean sauce (available from good supermarkets or Asian food stores)

a little vegetable oil

1 teaspoon sesame oil

2 x 250 g (8 oz) dough balls (see page 14)

⅔ cup (150 mL, 5 fl oz) Pizza Sauce (see page 16)

1¼ cups (150 g, 5 oz) grated mozzarella cheese

3 spring onions (scallions), sliced on the angle, Chinese style

½ cup (100 g, 3 oz) cashew nuts, roughly chopped

1½ cups (100 g, 3 oz) bean sprouts

¼ bunch of coriander (cilantro), freshly chopped

1 tablespoon sesame seeds, toasted

MAKES 2 MEDIUM PIZZAS

Marinate the beef in the blackbean sauce for at least 2 hours. Pour a little vegetable oil into a medium frying pan or wok. Add the sesame oil and heat until the oil begins to shimmer. Add the beef strips, taking care to avoid splashing yourself with the oil. Stir-fry for about 3 minutes, sealing the meat on all sides. Remove from the pan and allow to cool.

Place two pizza stones or tiles in the oven. Heat the oven to its highest possible setting (260°C/500°F/gas mark 10). Roll out the pizza dough, as described on page 16, so that you have two bases. Cover the bases with the Pizza Sauce and mozzarella cheese, keeping a 3 cm (1¼ in.) border around the edge of the dough clean.

Place the beef on the bases in a random pattern, leaving spaces for the other ingredients to fall into. Add the spring onion, cashews and bean sprouts. Sprinkle the coriander over the top.

Using a wide spatula or pizza paddle, gently slide each pizza onto a stone or tile. Cook for 10 minutes. Remove the pizzas from the oven when cooked and golden. Slice each pizza into eight pieces and serve immediately garnished with the sesame seeds.

# Marinated Lamb Fillets with Pesto

THIS PIZZA IS ESPECIALLY GOOD FOR THOSE OF YOU WHO ENJOY GARLIC-MARINATED LAMB ON A KEBAB-STYLE PIZZA.

3 teaspoons olive oil

1 teaspoon crushed garlic

300 g (10 oz) loin or backstrap lamb fillet (tenderloin), trimmed of any fat and sinew

2 x 250 g (8 oz) dough balls (see page 14)

⅔ cup (150 mL, 5 fl oz) Pizza Sauce (see page 16)

1¼ cups (150 g, 5 oz) grated mozzarella cheese

⅓ cup (100mL, 3 fl oz) Pesto Sauce (see page 19)

1 red capsicum (bell pepper), roasted, peeled and seeded, then cut into large chunks

freshly chopped basil

a little tabbouleh, or cucumber and yoghurt, to garnish (optional)

MAKES 2 MEDIUM PIZZAS

Combine the olive oil and garlic. Marinate the lamb in this mixture for several hours in the refrigerator.

Preheat the oven to 200°C (400°F/ gas mark 6). Heat a frying pan or skillet until quite hot. Add the lamb and quickly sear on all sides to seal in the juices (just long enough to colour the meat). Remove from the pan immediately.

Roast the lamb in the oven for about 5 minutes. (The cut of meat you use will dictate the length of the cooking time. As a general guide, the thicker the piece, the longer you will have to cook it. With lamb, the meat should still be pink; it is going back into the oven, so leave it slightly undercooked. If the lamb is cooked until rare now, it will be medium to rare once cooked on the pizza.) Alternatively, for extra flavour, cook the fillets on a char-grill or barbecue. Allow to cool and then cut into slices about ½ cm (¼ in.) thick. Set aside.

Place two pizza stones or tiles in the oven and increase the oven temperature to its highest possible setting (260°C/ 500°F/gas mark 10). Roll out the pizza dough, as described on page 16, so that you have two bases.

Cover the bases with the Pizza Sauce and mozzarella cheese, keeping a 3 cm (1¼ in.) border around the edge of the dough clean.

Place the lamb on the bases in a random pattern, leaving spaces for other ingredients to fall into. Using a teaspoon, dot small dollops of Pesto Sauce around each pizza. Add the roast capsicum and sprinkle some chopped basil over the top.

Using a wide spatula or pizza paddle, gently slide each pizza onto a stone or tile. Cook for 10 minutes. Remove the pizzas from the oven when cooked and golden. Slice each pizza into eight pieces. Serve immediately, garnished with the tabbouleh or cucumber and yoghurt (if using).

# Peperoni

~~~

DURING THE EVOLUTION OF THIS PIZZA, WE EXPERIMENTED WITH SEVERAL DIFFERENT TYPES OF PEPERONI. WE NOW USE A MIXTURE OF HOT AND MILD PEPERONI TO ACHIEVE A TASTY COMBINATION. SAMPLE A FEW DIFFERENT TYPES TO FIND THE COMBINATION YOU PREFER.

2 x 250 g (8 oz) dough balls
(see page 14)
⅔ cup (150 mL, 5 fl oz) Pizza Sauce
(see page 16)
1¼ cups (150 g, 5 oz) grated mozzarella
cheese
90 g (3 oz) peperoni, thinly sliced
150 g (5 oz) button mushrooms, thinly
sliced
½ cup (75 g, 2½ oz) kalamata olives,
pitted and cut into quarters
extra mozzarella cheese, grated

MAKES 2 MEDIUM PIZZAS

Place two pizza stones or tiles in the oven. Heat the oven to its highest possible setting (260°C/500°F/gas mark 10). Roll out the pizza dough, as described on page 16, so that you have two bases. Cover the bases with the Pizza Sauce and mozzarella cheese, keeping a 3 cm (1¼ in.) border around the edge of the dough clean.

Place the peperoni on the bases in a random pattern, leaving spaces for other ingredients to fall into. Add the mushrooms and olives. Sprinkle some extra mozzarella cheese over the top.

Using a wide spatula or pizza paddle, gently slide each pizza onto a stone or tile. Cook for 10 minutes. Remove the pizzas from the oven when cooked and golden. Slice each pizza into eight pieces and serve immediately.

OPPOSITE: *Grilled Chicken, Goat Cheese, Roast Peppers, Pine Nuts and Raisins (see page 46)*

# Spinach, Pancetta & Cashews with Feta

~~~~~

THE INTENSE FLAVOURS OF THE PANCETTA AND SUN-DRIED TOMATOES ARE CUT BY THE CREAMY FETA CHEESE, GIVING A FULL-BODIED PIZZA TOPPED WITH CRISP, ROASTED CASHEWS.

2 x 250 g (8 oz) dough balls
  (see page 14)
⅔ cup (150 mL, 5 fl oz) Pizza Sauce
  (see page 16)
1¼ cups (150 g, 5 oz) grated mozzarella
  cheese
30 g (1 oz) pancetta or prosciutto slices,
  cut into pieces about 3 cm x 1 cm
  (1¼ in. x ½ in.)
⅔ cup (40 g, 1½ oz) sun-dried tomatoes
  (drained of oil), cut into chunks
¼ cup (40 g, 1½ oz) unsalted roasted
  cashew nuts, roughly chopped
100 g (3 oz) feta cheese
16 baby spinach leaves, stems removed
  and leaves rubbed with a little olive
  oil

MAKES 2 MEDIUM PIZZAS

Place two pizza stones or tiles in the oven. Heat the oven to its highest possible setting (260°C/500°F/gas mark 10). Roll out the pizza dough, as described on page 16, so that you have two bases. Cover the bases with the Pizza Sauce and mozzarella cheese, keeping a 3 cm (1¼ in.) border around the edge of the dough clean.

Place the pancetta in a clock-style pattern around the edge of each base, with 2 pieces in the middle. Add the sun-dried tomatoes, cashews and feta. Place the spinach leaves over the top.

Using a wide spatula or pizza paddle, gently slide each pizza onto a stone or tile. Cook for 10 minutes. Remove the pizzas from the oven when cooked and golden. Slice each pizza into eight pieces and serve immediately.

OPPOSITE: *Spinach, Pancetta and Cashews with Feta (top) and Roast Beef, Sautéed Potato & Caramelised Onion with Bearnaise Sauce (bottom; see page 56).*

# Roast Beef, Sautéed Potato & Caramelised Onion with Bearnaise Sauce

~~~

A PERSONAL FAVOURITE. A PIZZA MAY NOT BE THE PLACE YOU EXPECT TO FIND ROAST FILLET OF BEEF, BUT IT IS A MOUTHWATERING TREAT. DON'T FORGET THE ALMOST OBLIGATORY GRINDS OF FRESH BLACK PEPPER.

**BEARNAISE SAUCE**

a little butter
1 brown (yellow) onion, finely diced
1 large sprig French tarragon, finely chopped
⅓ cup (90 mL, 3 fl oz) dry white wine
⅓ cup (90 mL, 3 fl oz) white wine vinegar
6 egg yolks
225 g (7 oz) butter, melted
salt, to taste
juice of ½ lemon
extra French tarragon, freshly chopped

a little olive oil
400 g (13 oz) beef tenderloin or sirloin
2 x 250 g (8 oz) dough balls (see page 14)
⅔ cup (150 mL, 5 fl oz) Pizza Sauce (see page 16)
1¼ cups (150 g, 5 oz) grated mozzarella cheese
4 medium potatoes, peeled and parboiled

1 Spanish (red) onion, cut into wedges and roasted (see page 20)
½ bunch of chives, chopped
freshly cracked black pepper, to taste

MAKES 2 MEDIUM PIZZAS

**BEARNAISE SAUCE**
Melt a little butter in a small saucepan and add the onion and French tarragon. Sauté until the onion is transparent and then add the white wine and vinegar. Bring to the boil over a medium heat and simmer gently until reduced in volume to about 3 tablespoons. Strain the liquid through a fine sieve.

Put the egg yolks in a medium stainless steel bowl and add the reduced liquid. Place a saucepan of warm water on the stove (the pan must be large enough for the stainless steel bowl to sit in, without the water touching the bottom of the bowl). Bring the water to a gentle simmer and place the bowl on top of the pan (this is known as a bain-marie or water bath). Reduce the heat under the water to very low.

Whisk the egg mixture continuously until it has doubled in size. Heat the melted butter and drizzle over the egg mixture, whisking constantly, until about four-fifths of the butter is incorporated. The sauce should now be nice and thick.

Season with a little salt and add the lemon juice and extra tarragon. Whisk thoroughly to combine and set aside until ready to use. (Only add the remaining melted butter if the sauce if still too thin after adding the lemon juice.)

Preheat the oven to 200°C (400°F/ gas mark 6). Heat a little olive oil in a frying pan or skillet until very hot. Add the beef and quickly sear on all sides to seal in the juices. Remove from the pan and roast in the oven for 5 minutes. Allow the beef to cool completely before slicing into pieces about ½ cm (¼ in.) thick. Set aside.

Place two pizza stones or tiles in the oven. Heat the oven to its highest possible setting (260°C/500°F/gas mark 10). Roll out the pizza dough, as described on page 16, so that you have two bases. Cover the bases with the Pizza Sauce and mozzarella cheese, keeping a 3 cm (1¼ in.) border around the edge of the dough clean.

Cut the potatoes into quarters. Sauté in a frying pan or skillet with a little olive oil until they are crisp and crunchy in texture. Place the potatoes on the bases in a random pattern, and then add the roast onion (the beef will go on the pizza halfway through cooking).

Using a wide spatula or pizza paddle, gently slide each pizza onto a stone or tile. Cook for 5 minutes. Now place the pieces of beef on the pizzas, and cook for a further 4 minutes. Remove the pizzas from the oven when cooked and golden. Slice each pizza into eight pieces. Spoon the Bearnaise Sauce generously over the top. Serve immediately garnished with the chives and seasoned with the black pepper.

# Hawaiian

~~~

A SIMPLE, TRIED AND TRUE COMBINATION THAT REMAINS POPULAR WITH ALL AGE GROUPS.

2 x 250 g (8 oz) dough balls
(see page 14)
⅔ cup (150 mL, 5 fl oz) Pizza Sauce
(see page 16)
1¾ cups (200 g, 7 oz) grated mozzarella
cheese
1 medium pineapple (about 300 g
(10 oz)), peeled and cut into 1 cm
(½ in.) cubes
200 g (7 oz) sliced double-smoked ham,
cut into strips ½ cm (¼ in.) wide and
3 cm (1¼ in.) long

MAKES 2 MEDIUM PIZZAS

Place two pizza stones or tiles in the oven. Heat the oven to its highest possible setting (260°C/500°F/gas mark 10). Roll out the pizza dough, as described on page 16, so that you have two bases. Cover the bases with the Pizza Sauce and 1¼ cups (150 g, 5 oz) of the mozzarella cheese, keeping a 3 cm (1¼ in.) border around the edge of the dough clean.

Place the pineapple on the bases in a random pattern, leaving gaps for the ham to fall into. Add the ham and sprinkle the remaining mozzarella cheese over the top.

Using a wide spatula or pizza paddle, gently slide each pizza onto a stone or tile. Cook for 10 minutes. Remove the pizzas from the oven when cooked and golden. Slice each pizza into eight pieces and serve immediately.

# Prosciutto with Eggplant & Sun-dried Tomatoes

~~~

THIS PIZZA IS AN ADVENTUROUS BUT SATISFYING COMBINATION OF SHARP,
ROBUST TASTES AND SUBTLE FLAVOURS.

1 medium eggplant (aubergine)
a little olive oil
salt and freshly ground black pepper,
  to taste
2 x 250 g (8 oz) dough balls
  (see page 14)
⅔ cup (150 mL, 5 fl oz) Pizza Sauce
  (see page 16)
1¼ cups (150 g, 5 oz) grated mozzarella
  cheese
⅔ cup (40 g, 1½ oz) sun-dried tomatoes
  (drained of oil), chopped
30 g (1 oz) sliced prosciutto, rind
  removed and cut into strips about
  3 cm (1¼ in.) wide
125 g (4 oz) goat cheese (such as
  Milawa), cut into chunks
1 tablespoon kalamata olives, pitted
  and cut into quarters
½ bunch of basil, freshly chopped

MAKES 2 MEDIUM PIZZAS

Preheat the oven to 160°C (325°F/gas mark 3). Slice the eggplant into pieces about 1 cm (½ in.) thick. Place the slices on a lightly oiled baking tray or sheet. Season with salt and pepper. Cover with greaseproof (wax) paper. Roast in the oven for 10–15 minutes or until soft. Cut any large pieces into halves or quarters.

Place two pizza stones or tiles in the oven. Heat the oven to its highest possible setting (260°C/500°F/gas mark 10). Roll out the pizza dough, as described on page 16, so that you have two bases. Cover the bases with the Pizza Sauce and mozzarella cheese, keeping a 3 cm (1¼ in.) border around the edge of the dough clean.

Place the sun-dried tomatoes on the bases first so that they do not burn. Add the eggplant in a random pattern, leaving spaces for other ingredients to fall into. Place the prosciutto on the pizzas. Add the goat cheese and olives. Sprinkle the basil over the top.

Using a wide spatula or pizza paddle, gently slide each pizza onto a stone or tile. Cook for 10 minutes. Remove from the oven when cooked and golden. Slice each pizza into eight. Serve immediately.

# Blackened Kangaroo with Cajun Seasoning

~~~~~~

KANGAROO IS A WONDERFULLY LEAN MEAT WITH A MILD GAMEY FLAVOUR,
MAKING IT AN IDEAL PARTNER FOR FIELD MUSHROOMS AND QUANDONGS (A FRUIT
NATIVE TO AUSTRALIA). IF QUANDONGS ARE UNAVAILABLE, SWEET POTATO MAKES
AN IDEAL SUBSTITUTE. LAMB FILLETS CAN BE USED IN PLACE OF KANGAROO.

a little oil

300 g (10 oz) kangaroo striploin or lamb fillets (tenderloin), rolled in Cajun seasoning to cover completely

40 g (1½ oz) quandongs, stone (pit) removed (simply increase quantity of sweet potato if quandongs are unavailable)

1 teaspoon white vinegar (if using quandongs)

2 x 250 g (8 oz) dough balls (see page 14)

⅔ cup (150 mL, 5 fl oz) Pizza Sauce (see page 16)

1¼ cups (150 g, 5 oz) grated mozzarella cheese

150 g (5 oz) mixed field or button mushrooms (such as oyster, flat, shimeji, enoki or shiitake), sliced

2 teaspoons olive oil

100 g (3 oz) red sweet potato or kumara, peeled and cut into slices ½ cm (¼ in.) thick, then roasted (see page 123)

½ bunch of small spinach leaves, stems removed

**CAJUN SEASONING**

2 tablespoons paprika

pinch of cayenne (red) pepper

1 teaspoon garlic powder

1 teaspoon ground white pepper

MAKES 2 MEDIUM PIZZAS

Preheat the oven to 200°C (400°F/gas mark 6). Heat the oil in a frying pan or skillet until almost smoking hot (this is important as the high temperature is needed to 'blacken' the meat). Add the kangaroo or lamb and quickly sear on all sides to 'blacken' the meat.

Transfer the meat to a roasting pan. Roast in the oven for about 5 minutes (like lamb, kangaroo is best cooked to rare). Allow the meat to cool, then slice into pieces ½ cm (¼ in.) thick.

Place the quandongs (if using) in a pan of cold water. Add the white vinegar. Bring to the boil and simmer gently for 15–20 minutes until cooked. Drain and set aside.

Meanwhile, place two pizza stones or tiles in the oven and increase the oven temperature to its highest possible setting (260°C/500°F/gas mark 10).

Roll out the pizza dough, as described on page 16, so that you have two bases. Cover the bases with the Pizza Sauce and mozzarella cheese, keeping a 3 cm (1¼ in.) border around the edge of the dough clean.

Put the mushrooms in a small bowl. Add the olive oil and toss through to coat the mushrooms. (This will help the mushrooms roast when they are baked on the pizza.) Place the sliced kangaroo on the bases in a random pattern, leaving spaces for other ingredients to fall into. Add the sweet potato, mushrooms, quandongs and spinach leaves.

Using a wide spatula or pizza paddle, gently slide each pizza onto a stone or tile. Cook for 10 minutes. Remove the pizzas from the oven when cooked and golden. Slice each pizza into eight pieces and serve immediately.

### CAJUN SEASONING

Combine the paprika, cayenne pepper, garlic powder and ground white pepper in a bowl. Mix thoroughly.

This seasoning will last indefinitely if stored in an airtight container.

# Spicy Lamb Sausage with Coriander

~~~

THIS PIZZA HAS A MIDDLE EASTERN FLAVOUR. USE A TASTY LAMB SAUSAGE FOR THE TOPPING, PERHAPS ONE CONTAINING GARLIC OR PAPRIKA, TO COMPLEMENT THE OTHER INGREDIENTS.

2 x 250 g (8 oz) dough balls
  (see page 14)
⅔ cup (150 mL, 5 fl oz) Pizza Sauce
  (see page 16)
1¼ cups (150 g, 5 oz) grated mozzarella
  cheese
200 g (7 oz) spicy (fresh) lamb sausage,
  sliced and seared in a frying pan or
  skillet
1 medium eggplant (aubergine), cut into
  slices ½ cm (¼ in.) thick and roasted
  (see page 123), then quartered
1 large red capsicum (bell pepper),
  roasted (see page 20) and cut into
  chunks
1 Spanish (red) onion, sliced into rings
¼ bunch of coriander (cilantro), freshly
  chopped

MAKES 2 MEDIUM PIZZAS

Place two pizza stones or tiles in the oven. Heat the oven to its highest possible setting (260°C/500°F/gas mark 10). Roll out the pizza dough, as described on page 16, so that you have two bases. Cover the bases with the Pizza Sauce and mozzarella cheese, keeping a 3 cm (1¼ in.) border around the edge of the dough clean.

Place the sausage slices on the bases in a random pattern. Add the eggplant and capsicum. Lay the onion rings over the top and sprinkle with the coriander.

Using a wide spatula or pizza paddle, gently slide each pizza onto a stone or tile. Cook for 10 minutes. Remove the pizzas from the oven when cooked and golden. Slice each pizza into eight pieces and serve immediately.

# Peperoni & Salami with Roast Pepper & Onion

~~~

EVEN THE MOST ADVENTUROUS PIZZA CONNOISSEURS ENJOY THE OCCASIONAL CLASSIC TOPPING COMBINATION SUCH AS THIS ONE. CHOOSE GOOD-QUALITY SPICY PEPERONI AND SALAMI FOR THIS PIZZA.

2 x 250 g (8 oz) dough balls
   (see page 14)
⅔ cup (150 mL, 5 fl oz) Pizza Sauce
   (see page 16)
1¼ cups (150 g, 5 oz) grated mozzarella
   cheese
60 g (2 oz) peperoni, sliced
60 g (2 oz) salami, sliced
1 red capsicum (bell pepper), roasted
   and cut into chunks (see page 20)
1 Spanish (red) onion, sliced into thin
   rings

MAKES 2 MEDIUM PIZZAS

Place two pizza stones or tiles in the oven. Heat the oven to its highest possible setting (260°C/500°F/gas mark 10). Roll out the pizza dough, as described on page 16, so that you have two bases. Cover the bases with the Pizza Sauce and mozzarella cheese, keeping a 3 cm (1¼ in.) border around the edge of the dough clean.

Place the peperoni and salami on the bases in a random pattern, leaving spaces for other ingredients to fall into. Add the roast capsicum and onion rings.

Using a wide spatula or pizza paddle, gently slide each pizza onto a stone or tile. Cook for 10 minutes. Remove the pizzas from the oven when cooked and golden. Slice each pizza into eight pieces and serve immediately.

# Spicy Mexican Beef with Jalapeños

~~~~~

THIS IS A TRADITIONAL-STYLE MEXICAN RECIPE WHERE THE BEEF IS SIMMERED OVER A LOW HEAT FOR 2–3 HOURS. THE 'FIRE' RATING OF THIS DISH IS HOT, BUT CAN BE TAMED DOWN TO SUIT YOUR TASTE IF YOU CAN'T STAND THE HEAT!

### SPICY MEXICAN BEEF

400 g (13 oz) sliced beef topside
   (top round steak), cut into strips
   about 3 cm (1¼ in.) long and 1 cm
   (½ in.) wide
salt, to taste
a little olive oil
1 brown (yellow) onion, diced
1 green capsicum (bell pepper), diced
½ teaspoon chilli paste
½ teaspoon crushed garlic
pinch each of ground cinnamon,
   cayenne (red) pepper and ground
   cloves
1 x 440 mL (14 fl oz) can crushed
   tomatoes
1 teaspoon malt or balsamic vinegar
1 tablespoon tomato paste (purée)
2 bay leaves
2 teaspoons sliced jalapeño chilli
   peppers, or to taste

2 x 250 g (8 oz) dough balls
   (see page 14)
3 cups (600 g, 1¼ lb) Spicy Mexican
   Beef (see above)
1¾ cups (200 g, 7 oz) grated mozzarella
   cheese

handful of corn chips, broken up
   roughly
3 spring onions (scallions), sliced on the
   angle, Chinese style
1 teaspoon dried chilli flakes
sour cream, to garnish

MAKES 2 MEDIUM PIZZAS

### SPICY MEXICAN BEEF

Put the sliced beef in a medium saucepan and add enough water to barely cover the meat. Season with salt. Bring to the boil and simmer gently over a medium heat until all the water has evaporated and the meat begins to cook in its own juices. This is a slow process, but it is most important to reduce the liquid gradually and gently.

Heat a little olive oil in a separate saucepan. Add the onion, capsicum, chilli paste, garlic, cinnamon, cayenne and cloves. Sauté until the onion is transparent. Add the crushed tomatoes, vinegar, tomato paste and bay leaves.

Add the meat and bring the mixture to the boil over a gentle heat. Stir thoroughly and then add the jalapeño chilli peppers. Remove from the heat and allow to cool before using. The meat should now have a shredded look and be broken down throughout the sauce.

Place two pizza stones or tiles in the oven. Heat the oven to its highest possible setting (260°C/500°F/gas mark 10). Roll out the pizza dough, as described on page 16, so that you have two bases.

Spoon the Spicy Mexican Beef directly onto the bases, keeping a 3 cm (1¼ in.) border around the edge of the dough clean. Top with 1¼ cups (150 g, 5 oz) of the mozzarella cheese. Sprinkle the corn chips and spring onions over the pizzas. Top with the remaining mozzarella. Now dust the dried chilli flakes over the top.

Using a wide spatula or pizza paddle, gently slide each pizza onto a stone or tile. Cook for 10 minutes. Remove the pizzas from the oven when cooked and golden. Slice each pizza into eight pieces and serve immediately, garnished with a dollop of sour cream.

# Aussie

~~~

A UNIQUELY AUSTRALIAN COMBINATION GARNISHED WITH TRADITIONAL BREAKFAST OR LUNCHTIME FARE.

2 x 250 g (8 oz) dough balls
(see page 14)

⅔ cup (150 mL, 5 fl oz) Pizza Sauce
(see page 16)

1¼ cups (150 g, 5 oz) grated mozzarella
cheese

2 lamb cutlets (Frenched rib chops)

200 g (7 oz) tomatoes, roasted
(see page 20)

150 g (5 oz) bacon, diced, cooked and
drained

1 medium Spanish (red) onion
(about 100 g, 3 oz), cut into wedges
and roasted (see page 20)

¼ bunch of lemon thyme leaves,
chopped

2 eggs

freshly cracked black pepper, to taste

MAKES 2 MEDIUM PIZZAS

Place two pizza stones or tiles in the oven. Heat the oven to its highest possible setting (260°C/500°F/gas mark 10). Roll out the pizza dough, as described on page 16, so that you have two bases. Cover the bases with the Pizza Sauce and mozzarella cheese, keeping a 3 cm (1¼ in.) border around the edge of the dough clean.

Cook the lamb cutlets in a small pan until they are just done. Set aside and keep warm.

Place the roast tomatoes on the bases in a random pattern, leaving spaces for other ingredients to fall into. Add the bacon and onion. Sprinkle the lemon thyme over the top.

Using a wide spatula or pizza paddle, gently slide each pizza onto a stone or tile. Cook for 10 minutes.

Meanwhile, fry the eggs in a nonstick frying pan or skillet. Set aside and keep warm.

Remove the pizzas from the oven when cooked and golden. Slice each pizza into eight pieces. Garnish each pizza with a fried egg and a lamb cutlet. Season with black pepper and serve immediately.

# Salami with Goat Cheese & Pesto

~~~

BIG FLAVOURS ROUNDED OUT WITH PESTO AND GOAT CHEESE MAKE FOR
A CLASSIC COMBINATION OF PIZZA INGREDIENTS.

2 x 250 g (8 oz) dough balls
   (see page 14)
⅔ cup (150 mL, 5 fl oz) Pizza Sauce
   (see page 16)
1¼ cups (150 g, 5 oz) grated mozzarella
   cheese
100 g (3 oz) salami, sliced
⅓ cup (100 mL, 3 fl oz) Pesto Sauce
   (see page 19)
1 red capsicum (bell pepper), roasted
   and cut into chunks (see page 20)
1½ tablespoons kalamata olives, pitted
   and cut into quarters
125 g (4 oz) goat cheese, cut into chunks

MAKES 2 MEDIUM PIZZAS

Place two pizza stones or tiles in the oven. Heat the oven to its highest possible setting (260°C/500°F/gas mark 10). Roll out the pizza dough, as described on page 16, so that you have two bases. Cover the bases with the Pizza Sauce and mozzarella cheese, keeping a 3 cm (1¼ in.) border around the edge of the dough clean.

Place the salami on the bases in a random pattern, leaving spaces for other ingredients to fall into. Using a teaspoon, place dollops of the Pesto Sauce on the pizzas. Add the capsicum, olives and goat cheese.

Using a wide spatula or pizza paddle, gently slide each pizza onto a stone or tile. Cook for 10 minutes. Remove the pizzas from the oven when cooked and golden. Slice each pizza into eight pieces and serve immediately.

# Grilled Lamb with Sweet Potato & Artichokes

~~~

THE CLASSIC INGREDIENTS LISTED HERE COULD WELL BE FROM A TRADITIONAL BAKED DINNER INSTEAD OF A PIZZA. THE SAUTÉED SWEET POTATO ADDS A NEW DIMENSION, BUT AN EXTREMELY TASTY ONE.

200 g (7 oz) lamb fillet (tenderloin), trimmed of any fat and sinew, then cut into pieces 3 cm (1½ in.) long

salt and freshly cracked black pepper, to taste

a little olive oil

2 x 250 g (8 oz) dough balls (see page 14)

⅔ cup (150 mL, 5 fl oz) Pizza Sauce (see page 16)

1¼ cups (150 g, 5 oz) grated mozzarella cheese

2 medium red sweet potatoes or kumara, cut into slices, cooked then sautéed in a little olive oil with some rosemary

1 cup (60 g, 2 oz) small oyster mushrooms, trimmed if necessary and rubbed with a little olive oil

2 marinated globe artichokes, halved then cut into quarters

1 tablespoon roast garlic purée (see page 21)

a few sprigs of rosemary

freshly cracked black pepper, to taste

MAKES 2 MEDIUM PIZZAS

Flatten the lamb pieces with a meat tenderiser or pounder, until they are about ½ cm (¼ in.) thick. Season with salt and pepper. Heat a little olive oil in a frying pan or skillet until quite hot. Add the lamb and quickly sear on all sides to seal in the juices (just long enough to colour the meat). Remove from the pan immediately. Set aside and allow to cool.

Place two pizza stones or tiles in the oven. Heat the oven to its highest possible setting (260°C/500°F/gas mark 10). Roll out the pizza dough, as described on page 16, so that you have two bases. Cover the bases with the Pizza Sauce and mozzarella cheese, keeping a 3 cm (1¼ in.) border around the edge of the dough clean.

Place the lamb on the bases in a random pattern, leaving spaces for other ingredients to fall into. Add the sweet potato, mushrooms, artichokes and garlic. Sprinkle the rosemary over the top.

Using a wide spatula or pizza paddle, gently slide each pizza onto a stone or tile. Cook for 10 minutes. Remove from the oven when cooked and golden. Slice each pizza into eight pieces and serve immediately, season70ed with black

# Supreme

~~~

THIS OLD STANDARD MAY BE A FIRM FAMILY FAVOURITE, BUT WHEN MADE
WITH THE FRESHEST OF INGREDIENTS IT TAKES ON A WHOLE NEW IDENTITY.
THIS IS AN EXTREMELY EASY PIZZA TO OVERLOAD WITH TOPPING, SO BE CAREFUL
NOT TO STACK IT WITH TOO MANY LAYERS AS THIS WILL PREVENT THE CHEESE
UNDERNEATH FROM MELTING.

2 x 250 g (8 oz) dough balls
(see page 14)

⅔ cup (150 mL, 5 fl oz) Pizza Sauce
(see page 16)

1¼ cups (150 g, 5 oz) grated mozzarella
cheese

125 g (4 oz) spicy lamb sausage, cut into
slices ½ cm (¼ in.) thick and seared in
a frying pan or skillet

125 g (4 oz) sliced double-smoked ham,
cut into small pieces

1 red capsicum (bell pepper), diced

10–15 button mushrooms, sliced and
rubbed with a little olive oil

1½ tablespoons kalamata olives, pitted
and cut into quarters

10 anchovy fillets, cut into pieces
(optional)

2–3 tablespoons grated mozzarella
cheese (extra)

MAKES 2 MEDIUM PIZZAS

Place two pizza stones or tiles in the
oven. Heat the oven to its highest possible
setting (260°C/500°F/gas mark 10).
Roll out the pizza dough, as described
on page 16, so that you have two bases.
Cover the bases with the Pizza Sauce
and mozzarella cheese, keeping a 3 cm
(1¼ in.) border around the edge of the
dough clean.

Place the sausage on the bases in
a random pattern. Next add the ham,
followed by the capsicum, mushrooms,
olives and anchovies (if using). Sprinkle
the extra mozzarella cheese over the top.

Using a wide spatula or pizza paddle,
gently slide each pizza onto a stone or
tile. Cook for 10 minutes. Remove the
pizzas from the oven when cooked and
golden. Slice each pizza into eight pieces
and serve immediately.

# Super Supreme

~~~

A HUGELY SATISFYING PIZZA FOR ALL TASTES AND AGES, FROM CHILDREN TO
ADULTS. FEEL FREE TO EXPERIMENT WITH EXTRA TOPPINGS TO SUIT INDIVIDUAL
TASTE, BUT BE CAREFUL NOT TO OVERLOAD THE PIZZA WITH TOO MANY
FLAVOURS OR TOO MANY INGREDIENTS.

2 x 250 g (8 oz) dough balls
(see page 14)
⅔ cup (150 mL, 5 fl oz) Pizza Sauce
(see page 16)
1¼ cups (150 g, 5 oz) grated mozzarella
cheese
40 g (1½ oz) peperoni, sliced
40 g (1½ oz) salami, sliced
100 g (3 oz) (fresh) sausage, cut into
slices ½ cm (¼ in.) thick and seared in
a frying pan or skillet
4 tomatoes (about 150 g (5 oz)), roasted
(see page 20) and cut into quarters
1 Spanish (red) onion, thinly sliced into
rings
10 button mushrooms, sliced and
rubbed with a little olive oil
1½ tablespoons green olives, pitted and
cut into quarters
2 teaspoons roast garlic purée
(see page 21)

MAKES 2 MEDIUM PIZZAS

Place two pizza stones or tiles in the
oven. Heat the oven to its highest possible
setting (260°C/500°F/gas mark 10).
Roll out the pizza dough, as described
on page 16, so that you have two bases.
Cover the bases with the Pizza Sauce
and mozzarella cheese, keeping a 3 cm
(1¼ in.) border around the edge of the
dough clean.

Place the peperoni, salami and
sausage on the bases in a random
pattern, leaving spaces for other
ingredients to fall into. Be careful not
to stack too many ingredients on top
of each other. Add the roast tomatoes,
onion rings, mushrooms and olives. Dot
the roast garlic over the top. You may like
to sprinkle a little extra mozzarella
cheese over the top to hold the
ingredients together.

Using a wide spatula or pizza paddle,
gently slide each pizza onto a stone or
tile. Cook for 10 minutes. Remove the
pizzas from the oven when cooked and
golden. Slice each pizza into eight pieces
and serve immediately.

OPPOSITE: *Super Supreme*

# Tex Mex

~~~

MINCED (GROUND) BEEF WITH PINTO BEANS IN A MILD TOMATO SAUCE MAKE
THIS A TASTY PIZZA, ESPECIALLY WHEN ENHANCED WITH SOUR CREAM
AND GUACAMOLE. A SIMPLE RECIPE FOR GUACAMOLE IS PROVIDED, BUT IF
TIME IS AGAINST YOU, THERE ARE MANY READY-MADE AVOCADO DIPS
AVAILABLE FROM YOUR SUPERMARKET.

## GUACAMOLE

2 avocados
½ Spanish (red) onion, diced
¼ bunch of coriander (cilantro), leaves
  picked and chopped
¼ teaspoon chilli paste, or to taste
juice of ½ lemon
juice of ½ lime
salt and freshly cracked black pepper,
  to taste

## TEX MEX SAUCE

1 tablespoon olive oil
1 onion, finely diced
1 green capsicum (bell pepper), finely
  diced
1 teaspoon chilli paste
1 teaspoon crushed garlic
350 g (11 oz) topside mince
  (ground beef)
1 x 440 mL (14 fl oz) can crushed
  tomatoes
¼ cup (60 mL, 2 fl oz) Barbecue Sauce
  (see page 19)
1 tablespoon tomato paste (purée)
1 x 150 g (5 oz) can cooked pinto or
  borlotti beans
salt and freshly ground black pepper,
  to taste

2 x 250 g (8 oz) dough balls
  (see page 14)
500 g (1 lb) Tex Mex Sauce (see above)
½ medium Spanish (red) onion, thinly
  sliced into rings
1¼ cups (150 g, 5 oz) grated mozzarella
  cheese
½ cup (125 mL, 4 fl oz) sour cream
½ cup (125 mL, 4 fl oz) Guacamole
  (see above)
large handful of corn chips

MAKES 2 MEDIUM PIZZAS

### GUACAMOLE

Halve and stone (pit) the avocados.
Peel and cut the flesh into large pieces.
Place in a bowl and add the remaining
ingredients. Mix thoroughly until smooth.
Store covered in the refrigerator until
needed.

OPPOSITE: *Tex Mex*

### TEX MEX SAUCE

Heat the olive oil in a medium saucepan. Add the onion, capsicum, chilli paste and garlic. Sauté until the onion is transparent. Add the mince, breaking it up with a wooden spoon as it browns so that it does not become lumpy. Simmer for 20 minutes.

Add the tomatoes, Barbecue Sauce and tomato paste. Simmer for another 10 minutes before adding the beans. Return to the boil and season with salt and pepper. Remove from the heat and allow to cool before using. The mixture will thicken to a heavy paste.

Place two pizza stones or tiles in the oven. Heat the oven to its highest possible setting (260°C/500°F/gas mark 10). Roll out the pizza dough, as described on page 16, so that you have two bases.

Spoon the Tex Mex Sauce onto the bases, keeping a 3 cm (1¼ in.) border around the edge of the dough clean. Sprinkle the mozzarella cheese over the top. Place the onion rings over each pizza in a random pattern.

Using a wide spatula or pizza paddle, gently slide each pizza onto a stone or tile. Cook for 10 minutes. Remove the pizzas from the oven when cooked and golden. Slice each pizza into eight pieces. Place a dollop each of sour cream and Guacamole in the centre of each pizza. Stand a few corn chips in the centre of each pizza. Serve immediately.

# Sausage with Cherry Tomatoes, Bacon & Mushrooms

~~~

SHOULD YOU FEEL LIKE A PIZZA FOR BREAKFAST, THIS IS TYPICAL MORNING FARE WITH A TWIST. THIS HEARTY TOPPING IS GUARANTEED TO GET YOUR ENGINE RUNNING!

2 x 250 g (8 oz) dough balls
  (see page 14)
⅔ cup (150 mL, 5 fl oz) Pizza Sauce
  (see page 16)
1¼ cups (150 g, 5 oz) grated mozzarella
  cheese
200 g (7 oz) (fresh) sausage of your
  choice, cut into slices ½ cm (¼ in.)
  thick and seared in a frying pan
  or skillet
125 g (4 oz) bacon rashers (slices), diced
  and cooked
½ punnet (125 g, 4 oz) cherry tomatoes,
  halved
12 button mushrooms, sliced and lightly
  oiled
3 spring onions (scallions), sliced on the
  angle, Chinese style

MAKES 2 MEDIUM PIZZAS

Place two pizza stones or tiles in the oven. Heat the oven to its highest possible setting (260°C/500°F/gas mark 10). Roll out the pizza dough, as described on page 16, so that you have two bases. Cover the bases with the Pizza Sauce and mozzarella cheese, keeping a 3 cm (1¼ in.) border around the edge of the dough clean.

Place the sausage on the bases in a random pattern, leaving spaces for other ingredients to fall into. Add the bacon, cherry tomatoes, mushrooms and spring onions. Sprinkle a little extra mozzarella cheese over the top if desired.

Using a wide spatula or pizza paddle, gently slide each pizza onto a stone or tile. Cook for 10 minutes. Remove the pizzas from the oven when cooked and golden. Slice each pizza into eight pieces and serve immediately.

# Ham, Broccoli & Almond with Dijon Mustard

~~~

THE BASE SAUCE FOR THIS PIZZA IS MADE WITH MASCARPONE AND DIJON
MUSTARD. THE FLAVOURS REMAIN SUBTLE, YET COMPLEMENT THE OTHER
INGREDIENTS PERFECTLY.

2 x 250 g (8 oz) dough balls
  (see page 14)
150 g (5 oz) mascarpone cheese
¼ cup (60 mL, 2 fl oz) Dijon mustard
1¼ cups (150 g, 5 oz) grated mozzarella
  cheese
2 heads broccoli, cut into florets and
  blanched
200 g (7 oz) sliced double-smoked ham,
  cut into strips or batons ½ cm (¼ in.)
  wide and 3 cm (1¼ in.) long
40 g (1½ oz) Brie cheese, cut into slices
  ½ cm (¼ in.) thick
1½–2 tablespoons sliced almonds

MAKES 2 MEDIUM PIZZAS

Place two pizza stones or tiles in the oven. Heat the oven to its highest possible setting (260°C/500°F/gas mark 10). Roll out the pizza dough, as described on page 16, so that you have two bases. Thoroughly combine the mascarpone cheese and Dijon mustard. Use this mixture to cover the bases, then sprinkle the mozzarella cheese over the top, keeping a 3 cm (1¼ in.) border from the edge of the dough clean.

Place the broccoli on the bases in a random pattern, leaving spaces for other ingredients to fall into. Add the ham. Break the slices of Brie into pieces 3 cm (1¼ in.) long and place on the pizza. Sprinkle the sliced almonds over the top.

Using a wide spatula or pizza paddle, gently slide each pizza onto a stone or tile. Cook for 10 minutes. Remove the pizzas from the oven when cooked and golden. Slice each pizza into eight pieces and serve immediately.

# Market
# CUISINE

THIS ASSORTMENT OF PIZZAS SHOWS YOU HOW
TO MAKE THE MOST OF SEASONALLY AVAILABLE
PRODUCE AND THE FRESHEST OF INGREDIENTS.

IN ESSENCE, THE BASE IS COOKED SEPARATELY WITH
ONLY SOME OF THE INGREDIENTS ON THE TOPPING.
MEANWHILE, THE MARKET CUISINE IS GRILLED, PAN-
FRIED OR ROASTED BEFORE BEING PLACED ON THE
PIZZA AT THE LAST MINUTE. AFTER GARNISHING
ACCORDINGLY, THE PIZZA IS BROUGHT TO THE
TABLE IMMEDIATELY.

THIS METHOD OF ASSEMBLY IS VERY SIMILAR IN
STYLE TO PRODUCING AN À LA CARTE MEAL, BUT
HERE THE PIZZA BASE IS USED AS THE VEHICLE
ON WHICH TO SERVE THE FOOD.

MOST OF THESE 'MARKET CUISINE' PIZZAS ARE BEST
MADE AS INDIVIDUAL SERVINGS, USING THE SAME
SIZE DOUGH BALL AS FOR THE MEDIUM PIZZAS, BUT
TRIMMED TO A DIAMETER OF 18 CM (7 IN.).

# Roast Flathead, Peppers, Bermuda Onions & Hazelnut Coriander Pesto

~~~

A MAGNIFICENT PIZZA OF JUST-COOKED FISH WITH PESTO DRIZZLED OVER THE TOP. THE FLATHEAD CAN BE REPLACED WITH ANY FIRM-FLESHED WHITE FISH. ALTHOUGH THE PESTO WILL LAST IN THE REFRIGERATOR FOR SOME TIME, IT IS BEST USED AS QUICKLY AS POSSIBLE AS THE DELICATE CORIANDER BOUQUET DETERIORATES RAPIDLY.

**HAZELNUT CORIANDER PESTO**
⅔ cup (about 2 handfuls) coriander (cilantro) leaves
¼ cup (about 1 small handful) chopped chives
1 tablespoon shelled and roasted hazelnuts
1 clove garlic
1⅛ tablespoons olive oil
1 tablespoon grated Parmesan cheese

2 x 250 g (8 oz) dough balls (see page 14)
⅓ cup (90 mL, 3 fl oz) Pizza Sauce (see page 16)
¾ cup (100 g, 3 oz) grated mozzarella cheese
1 red capsicum (bell pepper), roasted, peeled and diced (see page 20)
1 Bermuda or Spanish (red) onion, cut into wedges and roasted (see page 20)
a little olive oil

4 medium flathead or flounder fillets (about 440 g (14 oz)), skinned and boned

MAKES 2 INDIVIDUAL PIZZAS

**HAZELNUT CORIANDER PESTO**
Put the coriander, chives, hazelnuts and garlic in an electric blender or food processor. Blend or process until finely chopped. With the motor running, slowly add the oil and Parmesan cheese. Blend into a smooth purée. Transfer to a bowl, cover and set aside until needed. (If you are not making your pizza immediately, refrigerate the pesto until needed.)

Place two pizza stones or tiles in the oven. Heat the oven to its highest possible setting (260°C/500°F/gas mark 10). Roll out the pizza dough, as described on page 16, so that you have two bases.

Find a plate approximately 18 cm (7 in.) in diameter and place it face down on one of the bases. Take a sharp knife and run it around the outside of the plate to cut a smaller base. Remove the plate. You should now have a round, smooth-edged base. Repeat with the other base.

Cover the bases with the Pizza Sauce and mozzarella cheese, keeping a 1 cm (½ in.) border around the edge of the dough clean. Place the capsicum and onion on the bases in a random pattern.

Using a wide spatula or pizza paddle, gently slide each pizza onto a stone or tile. Cook for 8 minutes.

Meanwhile, heat a little olive oil in a nonstick frying pan or skillet over a moderate heat. When the oil is shimmering, add the fish to the pan. Let it start to colour and then turn. Continue cooking until the other side has started to colour. Remove from the pan. Your pizzas should be ready now.

Remove the pizzas from the oven when cooked and golden. Slice each pizza into four pieces. Place the pizzas on serving plates before assembling. Add the fish pieces in a random pattern. Drizzle the pesto all over the pizzas and serve immediately.

# Pancetta, Asparagus, Spinach & Poached Egg

~~~

ADDING A SOFT POACHED EGG ALMOST TURNS THIS PIZZA INTO BREAKFAST FARE. THE SPINACH IS RAW WHEN PLACED ON THE TOPPING, BUT THE COMBINED HEAT OF THE PIZZA AND THE POACHED EGG MEANS THAT IT QUICKLY COOKS.

1 bunch of asparagus
2 x 250 g (8 oz) dough balls
(see page 14)
⅓ cup (90 mL, 3 fl oz) Pizza Sauce
(see page 16)
¾ cup (100 g, 3 oz) grated mozzarella
cheese
20 g (¾ oz) sliced pancetta
2 eggs
12–15 baby spinach leaves, rinsed and
stems removed
freshly cracked black pepper, to taste

MAKES 2 INDIVIDUAL PIZZAS

Peel the bottom two-thirds of the stems of the asparagus. Steam or poach the spears in hot water for 2–3 minutes until just done. Plunge into icy cold water to stop the asparagus cooking any further. Drain when cool. Cut the thicker stems in half lengthways and trim the spears into pieces about 5 cm (2 in.) long. Set aside.

Place two pizza stones or tiles in the oven. Heat the oven to its highest possible setting (260°C/500°F/gas mark 10). Roll out the pizza dough, as described on page 16, so that you have two bases. Find a plate approximately 18 cm (7 in.) in diameter and place it face down on one of the bases. Take a sharp knife and run it around the outside of the plate to cut a smaller base. Remove the plate. You should now have a round, smooth-edged base. Repeat with the other base.

Cover the bases with the Pizza Sauce and mozzarella cheese, keeping a 1 cm (½ in.) border around the edge of the dough clean. Place the asparagus spears on the bases in a clock-style pattern, with the spears pointing outward from the centre of each pizza. Add the pancetta, allowing one piece per slice and one for the middle of each pizza.

Using a wide spatula or pizza paddle, gently slide each pizza onto a stone or tile. Cook for 8 minutes. Meanwhile, gently poach the eggs for 3–4 minutes. Remove the pizzas from the oven when cooked and golden. Slice each pizza into four pieces. Place the pizzas on serving plates before assembling. Put a small pile of spinach leaves in the centre of each pizza. Top with a poached egg. Garnish with black pepper and serve immediately.

# Niçoise Pizza with Tuna

~~~

A FABULOUS PIZZA THAT IS ESPECIALLY DELICIOUS WHEN SERVED IN THE
WARMER MONTHS OF THE YEAR WHEN TUNA, GREEN BEANS AND TOMATOES
REACH THEIR SEASONAL PEAK.

2 x 250 g (8 oz) dough balls
  (see page 14)
⅓ cup (90 mL, 3 fl oz) Pizza Sauce
  (see page 16)
¾ cup (100 g, 3 oz) grated mozzarella
  cheese
8 kalamata olives, pitted and halved
1 medium potato, peeled and boiled
4 cherry tomatoes, halved
40 g (1½ oz) feta cheese, diced
250 g (8 oz) tuna fillet or steaks
salt and freshly ground black pepper,
  to taste
60 g (2 oz) green (French, string) beans,
  blanched and cut into 3 cm (1¼ in.)
  pieces
juice of ½ lemon

MAKES 2 INDIVIDUAL PIZZAS

Place two pizza stones or tiles in the
oven. Heat the oven to its highest possible
setting (260°C/500°F/gas mark 10).
Roll out the pizza dough, as described
on page 16, so that you have two bases.
Find a plate approximately 18 cm (7 in.)
in diameter and place it face down on
one of the bases. Take a sharp knife and
run it around the outside of the plate to
cut a smaller base. Remove the plate. You
should now have a round, smooth-edged
base. Repeat with the other base.

Cover the bases with the Pizza Sauce
and mozzarella cheese, keeping a 1 cm
(½ in.) border around the edge of the
dough clean. Place the olives on the
bases in a random pattern. Cut the
potato into quarters and slice. Add to
the bases with the cherry tomatoes and
feta cheese. Using a wide spatula or
pizza paddle, gently slide each pizza
onto a stone or tile. Cook for 8 minutes.

Meanwhile, place the tuna on a lightly
oiled tray and season with salt and
pepper. Char-grill or barbecue by quickly
searing on both sides. (Alternatively,
quickly sear on both sides in a frying pan
or skillet). Carefully slice the tuna into
strips ½ cm (¼ in.) wide. Place the tuna
and green beans on a plate and drizzle
with the lemon juice. Your pizzas should
be ready now.

Remove the pizzas from the oven
when cooked and golden. Slice each
pizza into four pieces. Place the pizzas
on serving plates before assembling.
Spoon the tuna and beans over the
pizzas. Drizzle with any leftover lemon
juice and serve immediately.

# Togarashi Beef

～～～

FOR THIS HOT AND SPICY JAPANESE-SEASONED PIZZA, THE BEEF IS COATED IN
TOGARASHI SEASONING AND THEN WOK-CHARRED.

250 g (8 oz) beef rump or sirloin, cut
  into small strips about 3 cm x 1 cm
  (1¼ in. x ½ in.)
2 teaspoons togarashi seasoning
  (available from Asian or gourmet
  stores)
4 large cap or field mushrooms, peeled
  if necessary and cut into slices 2 cm
  (½ in.) thick
2 x 250 g (8 oz) dough balls
  (see page 14)
⅓ cup (90 mL, 3 fl oz) Pizza Sauce
  (see page 16)
¾ cup (100 g, 3 oz) grated mozzarella
  cheese
2 spring onions (scallions), finely sliced
a little sesame oil
1 small carrot, cut into very fine
  julienne about 3 cm (1¼ in.) long
a few coriander (cilantro) leaves,
  to garnish

MAKES 2 INDIVIDUAL PIZZAS

Marinate the beef in the togarashi
seasoning for at least 2 hours.

Grill or barbecue the mushrooms until
they start to colour. Turn and cook on the
other side. Alternatively, sauté in a little
butter in a frying pan or skillet. Remove
from the pan and drain. Set aside.

Place two pizza stones or tiles in the
oven. Heat the oven to its highest possible
setting (260°C/500°F/gas mark 10).
Roll out the pizza dough, as described
on page 16, so that you have two bases.
Find a plate approximately 18 cm (7 in.)
in diameter and place it face down on
one of the bases. Take a sharp knife and
run it around the outside of the plate to
cut a smaller base. Remove the plate. You
should now have a round, smooth-edged
base. Repeat with the other base.

Cover the bases with the Pizza Sauce
and mozzarella cheese, keeping a 1 cm
(½ in.) border around the edge of the
dough clean. Place the mushrooms on
the bases. Sprinkle the spring onion over
the top. Using a wide spatula or pizza
paddle, gently slide each pizza onto
a stone or tile. Cook for 8 minutes.

Halfway through the cooking time,
heat the sesame oil in a wok or frying
pan over a high heat. When the oil is
almost smoking, add the beef and carrot.
Stir-fry for about 2 minutes, to seal the
meat. Remove from the wok and drain.

Remove the pizzas from the oven
when cooked and golden. Slice each
pizza into four pieces. Place on serving
plates before assembling. Spoon the beef
and carrot onto the pizzas. Garnish with
the coriander and serve immediately.

# Grilled Yabbies, Roma Tomatoes & Oregano Pesto

FRESH YABBIES COMPLEMENTED WITH FLAVOURS TYPICAL OF TUSCANY
SEEM TO MAKE THIS PIZZA ALMOST IRRESISTIBLE.

## OREGANO PESTO

2 large red capsicums (bell peppers)
  roasted, peeled and seeded
  (see page 20)
¼ cup (45 g, 1½ oz) pine nuts, toasted
3 large cloves garlic, roasted and peeled
  (see page 21)
large handful of oregano, freshly
  chopped
¼ cup (60 mL, 2 fl oz) virgin olive oil
3 tablespoons Parmesan cheese shavings

2 x 250 g (8 oz) dough balls
  (see page 14)
⅔ cup (150 mL, 5 fl oz) Pizza Sauce
  (see page 16)
1¼ cups (150 g, 5 oz) grated mozzarella
  cheese
1 large red capsicum (bell pepper),
  roasted, peeled, seeded and cut into
  chunks (see page 20)
8 small Roma (egg, plum) tomatoes,
  halved and roasted (see page 20)
a few oregano leaves, freshly chopped
16 fresh green yabbies or marron,
  cleaned, or prawns (shrimp), peeled
  and deveined

MAKES 2 MEDIUM PIZZAS

## OREGANO PESTO

Blend or process the roast capsicum, pine nuts, roast garlic and oregano until finely chopped. Add the virgin olive oil and Parmesan cheese. Blend until smooth.

Cut the yabbies or marron in half lengthways. Rinse under cold, running water to remove mustard from the meat.

Place two pizza stones or tiles in the oven. Heat the oven to its highest possible setting (260°C/500°F/gas mark 10). Roll out the dough, as described on page 16, so that you have two bases. Cover with the Pizza Sauce and mozzarella cheese, keeping a 3 cm (1⅓ in.) border around the edge of the dough clean.

Place the roast tomato and roast capsicum on each of the bases. Sprinkle the oregano over the top. Using a wide spatula or pizza paddle, gently slide each pizza onto a stone or tile. Cook for 10 minutes. Meanwhile, lightly char-grill or barbecue the shellfish on both sides. Remove the pizzas from the oven when cooked and golden. Slice each pizza into eight pieces and place a shellfish on each slice. Spoon the Oregano Pesto over the top and serve immediately.

# Open Souvlaki

~~~

THIS PIZZA WAS THE PIONEER OF ALL OUR MARKET CUISINE CREATIONS AND IT STILL HAS A HIGH FOLLOWING AMONG OUR LUNCHTIME CLIENTELE. THE BEST WAY TO COOK THE LAMB IS ON THE BARS OF A VERY HOT BARBECUE OR CHAR-GRILL. IF YOU DON'T HAVE EITHER OF THESE, USE A VERY HOT FRYING PAN OR SKILLET, AND SIMPLY SEAR THE MEAT ON EACH SIDE.

1 backstrap or loin of lamb, about 375 g (12 oz), trimmed of any fat and skin
a little olive oil
2 cloves garlic, crushed
2 x 250 g (8 oz) dough balls (see page 14)
⅓ cup (90 mL, 3 fl oz) Pizza Sauce (see page 16)
¾ cup (100 g, 3 oz) grated mozzarella cheese
1 red capsicum (bell pepper), roasted, peeled, seeded and cut into dice (see page 20)
90 g (3 oz) herb and garlic boursin (cream cheese), cut into large chunks
2 handfuls baby mixed leaves or mesclun, rinsed and dried
¼ cup tabbouleh (see below)
a little balsamic vinegar
a little olive oil
freshly cracked black pepper, to taste

MAKES 2 INDIVIDUAL PIZZAS

Cut the lamb into slices 1 cm (½ in.) thick. You should have 10–12 slices. Tenderise the lamb with a meat hammer. Marinate in a little olive oil with the crushed garlic.

Place two pizza stones or tiles in the oven. Heat the oven to its highest possible setting (260°C/500°F/gas mark 10). Roll out the pizza dough, as described on page 16, so that you have two bases. Find a plate approximately 18 cm (7 in.) in diameter and place it face down on one of the bases. Take a sharp knife and run it around the outside of the plate to cut a smaller base. Remove the plate. You should now have a round, smooth-edged base. Repeat with the other base.

Cover the bases with the Pizza Sauce and mozzarella cheese, keeping a 1 cm (½ in.) border around the edge of the dough clean. Place the capsicum and boursin on the bases in a random pattern.

Using a wide spatula or pizza paddle, gently slide each pizza onto a stone or tile. Cook for 8 minutes.

Meanwhile, quickly sear the lamb slices on both sides on the bars of a very hot barbecue (use a very hot frying pan or skillet if you do not have a barbecue).

Do not overcook the lamb; simply seal the meat on each side. Your pizzas should be ready now.

Remove the pizzas from the oven when cooked and golden. Slice each pizza into four pieces. Place the pizzas on serving plates before assembling. Lay the lamb slices around the border of the topping, with one slice in the middle. Place a small pile of mixed leaves or mesclun in the centre of each pizza (on top of the lamb). Spoon the tabbouleh over the top of the mixed leaves. Drizzle each pizza with a few drops of balsamic vinegar and a little olive oil. Season with black pepper and serve immediately.

## TABBOULEH

Cut 1 tomato into wedges and discard the seeds. Cut the tomato flesh into dice. Combine the tomato with 1 tablespoon cooked couscous and 1 tablespoon chopped flat-leaf (Italian) parsley. Set aside until ready to use.

If you do not have the time to prepare your own tabbouleh for this pizza, you can use a good-quality store-bought one instead.

# Baby Octopus, Eggplant, Roast Peppers & Sweet Basil Oil

~~~

THIS PIZZA FEATURES BABY OCTOPUS, PILED HIGH ON A NEST OF MEDITERRANEAN VEGETABLES, AND THEN DRIZZLED WITH A FRUITY, BASIL-INFUSED OLIVE OIL. THE OCTOPUS SHOULD BE CHARRED ON A BARBECUE TO BRING OUT THE BEST FLAVOUR.

## SWEET BASIL OIL
½ large bunch of basil
2 whole cloves garlic. roasted
  (see page 21)
1 cup (250 mL, 8 fl oz) virgin olive oil
1 cup (250 mL, 8 fl oz) olive oil

350 g (11 oz) baby octopus, beak and
  eyes removed, trimmed and cleaned
grated zest and juice of 1 lemon
1 tablespoon olive oil
salt and freshly cracked black pepper,
  to taste

2 x 250 g (8 oz) dough balls
  (see page 14)
⅔ cup (150 mL, 5 fl oz) Pizza Sauce
  (see page 16)
1¼ cups (150 g, 5 oz) grated mozzarella
  cheese
1 large eggplant (aubergine), cut into
  slices ½ cm (¼ in.) thick, roasted
  (see page 123)

1 large red capsicum (bell pepper),
  roasted, peeled and cut into chunks
  (see page 20)
2 spring onions (scallions), sliced on the
  angle, Chinese style
1 tablespoon Sweet Basil Oil (see
  opposite) or extra virgin olive oil

MAKES 2 MEDIUM PIZZAS

## SWEET BASIL OIL
Place the basil, roast garlic, virgin olive oil and olive oil in a jar. Make sure that the basil is completely submerged, otherwise it may become mouldy. Seal the jar and let stand in a cool, dark place for at least 1 week before using. This oil will last indefinitely if stored in the refrigerator.

Place the baby octopus in a shallow container. Add the lemon zest and juice, and the olive oil. Season with salt and pepper. Leave to marinate while preparing the rest of the pizza.

Place two pizza stones or tiles in the oven. Heat the oven to its highest possible setting (260°C/500°F/gas mark 10). Roll out the pizza dough, as described on page 16, so that you have two bases. Cover the bases with the Pizza Sauce and mozzarella cheese, keeping a 3 cm (1⅓ in.) border around the edge of the dough clean.

Cut the roast eggplant into chunks. Place on each of the bases in a random pattern. Add the roast capsicum. Sprinkle the spring onions over the top. Using a wide spatula or pizza paddle, gently slide each pizza onto a stone or tile. Cook for 10 minutes.

Meanwhile, sear the baby octopus on a barbecue or char-grill. Allow to char lightly and the ends to become crisp before turning to cook on the other side.

Remove the pizzas from the oven when cooked and golden. Slice each pizza into eight pieces. Pile the baby octopus in the centre of each pizza. Drizzle with the Sweet Basil Oil and serve immediately.

# Duck Sausage, Pistachios, Sweet Potato & Sage

~~~

A SPECIALISED BUTCHER OR CHARCUTERIE WILL STOCK THE SAUSAGES NEEDED FOR THIS PIZZA, BUT FEEL FREE TO REPLACE THEM WITH ANOTHER VARIETY, SUCH AS COTECHINO, LOUKANIKA OR CHORIZO.

4 medium to large duck or other fresh
  sausages
2 x 250 g (8 oz) dough balls
  (see page 14)
⅔ cup (150 mL, 5 fl oz) Pizza Sauce
  (see page 16)
1½ cups (185 g, 6 oz) grated mozzarella
  cheese
1 medium sweet potato or kumara, cut
  into slices ½ cm (¼ in.) thick and
  roasted (see page 123)
1 medium Spanish (red) onion, cut into
  wedges and roasted (see page 20)
2 teaspoons chopped pistachio nuts
a few fresh sage leaves, freshly chopped
  (do not chop the leaves until you are
  ready to use them or they will lose
  their fragrance and flavour)

MAKES 2 MEDIUM PIZZAS

OPPOSITE: *Ham, Broccoli and Almonds
with Dijon Mustard (see page 76)*

Blanch the sausages in boiling water for several minutes. Sauté in a frying pan or skillet over a medium heat for 8–10 minutes. Allow to cool. Cut into slices 1 cm (½ cm) thick. Set aside.

Place two pizza stones or tiles in the oven. Heat the oven to its highest possible setting (260°C/500°F/gas mark 10). Roll out the pizza dough, as described on page 16, so that you have two bases. Cover the bases with the Pizza Sauce and 1⅓ cups (150 g, 5 oz) of the mozzarella cheese, keeping a 3 cm (1⅓ in.) border around the edge of the dough clean.

Place the sausage on each of the bases in a random pattern. Add the sweet potato, roast onion and pistachio nuts. Scatter the remaining mozzarella cheese over the pizzas. Sprinkle the sage over the top.

Using a wide spatula or pizza paddle, gently slide each pizza onto a stone or tile. Cook for 10 minutes. Remove the pizzas from the oven when cooked and golden. Slice each pizza into eight pieces and serve immediately.

# Primavera

〜〜〜

THIS IS A VERY SIMPLE PIZZA BASED ON AN ITALIAN PRIMAVERA
OR SPRING PIE. ASPARAGUS, FRESH PEAS, GREEN BEANS AND CHERRY
TOMATOES — ALL PLENTIFUL IN THE MARKETS WHEN THEY ARE IN SEASON —
ARE COMPLEMENTED BY ROMANO CHEESE.

¾ cup (100 g, 3 oz) shelled fresh green
  peas
⅔ cup (100 g, 3 oz) fine green
  (French, string) beans
12 spears young asparagus
2 x 250 g (8 oz) dough balls
  (see page 14)
⅔ cup (150 mL, 5 fl oz) Pizza Sauce
  (see page 16)
1¼ cups (150 g, 5 oz) grated mozzarella
  cheese
10 cherry tomatoes, halved
½ cup (100 g.3 oz) freshly shaved
  Romano cheese
½ small handful of basil leaves, freshly
  chopped
freshly cracked black pepper, to taste

MAKES 2 MEDIUM PIZZAS

Blanch the peas, green beans and
asparagus in separate small saucepans of
boiling water until just cooked. Be careful
not to overcook the vegetables as they
must retain their crispness and vibrant
colours. Refresh in icy cold water. Allow
to drain. Cut the green beans and
asparagus into 3 cm (1¼ in.) lengths.

Place two pizza stones or tiles in the
oven. Heat the oven to its highest possible
setting (260°C/500°F/gas mark 10).
Roll out the pizza dough, as described
on page 16, so that you have two bases.
Cover the bases with the Pizza Sauce
and mozzarella cheese, keeping a 3 cm
(1⅓ in.) border around the edge of the
dough clean.

Place the cherry tomatoes on each of
the bases in a random pattern. Spoon the
peas over the top. Add the green beans
and asparagus. Scatter the Romano
cheese over the pizzas and sprinkle with
the basil.

Using a wide spatula or pizza paddle,
gently slide each pizza onto a stone or
tile. Cook for 10 minutes. Remove the
pizzas from the oven when cooked and
golden. Slice each pizza into eight pieces
and serve immediately, seasoned with the
black pepper.

OPPOSITE: *Grilled Lamb with Sweet
Potato and Artichokes (see page 68)*

# Smoked Trout, Bok Choy & Enoki Mushrooms

~~~

A DELICATELY FLAVOURED PIZZA WITH SUBTLE TASTES THAT MELD
TO FORM A UNIQUE EAST-WEST COMBINATION.

1 bunch of bok choy (Chinese white
  cabbage)
1 spring onion (scallion) finely sliced
2 teaspoons grated ginger
150 g (5 oz) smoked trout, sliced and
  cut into strips about 1 cm (½ in.) wide
2 teaspoons medium-sweet soy sauce
freshly cracked black pepper, to taste
2 x 250 g (8 oz) dough balls
  (see page 14)
⅓ cup (90 mL, 3 fl oz) Pizza Sauce
  (see page 16)
¾ cup (100 g, 3 oz) grated mozzarella
  cheese
8 teardrop (pear) tomatoes, halved
250 g (8 oz) enoki mushrooms, stems
  discarded
a little olive oil
4 basil leaves, sliced
½ teaspoon sesame seeds

MAKES 2 INDIVIDUAL PIZZAS

Blanch the bok choy in boiling water until
just cooked. Refresh in icy cold water. Pat
dry and slice into fine strips. Place the
bok choy, spring onion, ginger, smoked
trout and soy sauce in a bowl. Mix
thoroughly. Season with pepper.

Place two pizza stones or tiles in the
oven. Heat the oven to its highest possible
setting (260°C/500°F/gas mark 10).
Roll out the pizza dough, as described
on page 16, so that you have two bases.
Find a plate approximately 18 cm (7 in.)
in diameter and place it face down on
one of the bases. Take a sharp knife and
run it around the outside of the plate to
cut a smaller base. Remove the plate. You
should now have a round, smooth-edged
base. Repeat with the other base.

Cover the bases with the Pizza Sauce
and mozzarella cheese, keeping a 1 cm
(½ in.) border around the edge of the
dough clean. Place a thin layer of the
bok choy mixture over the top. Add the
teardrop tomatoes. Using a wide spatula
or pizza paddle, gently slide each pizza
onto a stone or tile. Cook for 8 minutes.

Meanwhile, heat a little olive oil in a
frying pan or skillet. Add the mushrooms.
Sauté for 2–3 minutes. Stir the basil and
sesame seeds through the mushrooms.

Remove the pizzas from the oven
when cooked and golden. Slice each
pizza into four pieces. Place the pizzas
on serving plates. Spoon the mushrooms
over the top and serve immediately.

# Fruits of the
# SEA

WITH SUCH AN ARRAY OF PLENTIFUL MORSELS
TO CHOOSE FROM, WITH OR WITHOUT SHELLS,
SEAFOOD MAKES A SUPERB PIZZA TOPPING. THE
FLAVOURS OF SEAFOOD ARE DELICATE AND THE MEAT
IS SWEET. PARTNERED INGREDIENTS SHOULD ALWAYS
BE POLITE IN TASTE, COMPLEMENTING RATHER THAN
DROWNING OUT SEAFOOD'S SUBTLE FLAVOURS.

ALWAYS SELECT THE FRESHEST FISH AND SHELLFISH.
COOK IT QUICKLY TO SEAL IN THE JUICES. STIR-
FRYING, BARBECUING AND STEAMING — ALL FAST
METHODS OF COOKING — ARE THE MOST SUITABLE.
MOST IMPORTANTLY, NEVER OVERCOOK SEAFOOD.

# Tuscan

~~~

THIS PIZZA COMBINES THE FLAVOURS OF SELECT SEAFOOD WITH THOSE
OF TOMATO, GARLIC AND BASIL TO PRODUCE THE TASTE OF TUSCANY.

2 x 250 g (8 oz) dough balls
  (see page 14)
⅔ cup (150 mL, 5 fl oz) Pizza Sauce
  (see page 16)
1¾ cups (225 g, 7 oz) grated mozzarella
  cheese
100 g (3 oz) mussels, cooked
  (see page 12)
12 prawns (shrimp), cooked, peeled
  and deveined
100 g (3 oz) scallops, cooked
  (see page 12)
4 small to medium tomatoes (about
  200 g (7 oz)), roasted (see page 20)
2 tablespoons roast garlic purée
  (see page 21)
½ bunch of basil, finely sliced
freshly cracked black pepper, to taste

MAKES 2 MEDIUM PIZZAS

Place two pizza stones or tiles in the oven. Heat the oven to its highest possible setting (260°C/500°F/gas mark 10). Roll out the pizza dough, as described on page 16, so that you have two bases. Cover the bases with the Pizza Sauce and mozzarella cheese (reserve some cheese for topping the pizza), keeping a 3 cm (1¼ in.) border around the edge of the dough clean.

Distribute the seafood evenly over each base in a clock-style pattern, placing the mussels, prawns and scallops alternately. Place any leftover seafood in the centre of the pizza in a similar pattern. Add the tomato and dollops of the roast garlic, placing all over the pizzas. Sprinkle the extra cheese and the basil over the top.

Using a wide spatula or pizza paddle, gently slide each pizza onto a stone or tile. Cook for 10 minutes. Remove the pizzas from the oven when cooked and golden. Slice each pizza into eight pieces and serve immediately, garnished with the black pepper.

# Cajun Scallops

~~~

YOU WILL NEED CAJUN SEASONING FOR THIS SOUTHERN-STYLE PIZZA. YOU MAY BE ABLE TO BUY THIS, BUT I HAVE GIVEN A SIMPLE RECIPE FOR MAKING YOUR OWN ON PAGE 60. ONCE YOU HAVE, IT WILL LAST INDEFINITELY.

2 x 250 g (8 oz) dough balls
(see page 14)

⅔ cup (150 mL, 5 fl oz) Pizza Sauce
(see page 16)

1¼ cups (150 g, 5 oz) grated mozzarella
cheese

250 g (8 oz) scallops, dusted in Cajun
seasoning (see pages 60–1) and
seared on both sides in a very hot
pan (see page 12 for notes on cooking
seafood)

150 g (5 oz) red sweet potato or
kumara, cut into slices ½ cm (¼ in.)
thick and roasted in a moderate
oven at 160°C (325°F/gas mark 3)
for 12–15 minutes or until cooked

1 medium Spanish (red) onion (about
100 g (3 oz)), cut into wedges and
roasted (see page 20)

1 red capsicum (bell pepper), roasted
and cut into chunks (see page 20)

½ bunch of chives, finely sliced

MAKES 2 MEDIUM PIZZAS

Place two pizza stones or tiles in the oven. Heat the oven to its highest possible setting (260°C/500°F/gas mark 10). Roll out the pizza dough, as described on page 16, so that you have two bases. Cover the bases with the Pizza Sauce and mozzarella cheese, keeping a 3 cm (1¼ in.) border around the edge of the dough clean.

Distribute the scallops evenly over each base in a clock-style pattern. Place any leftover scallops in the centre of each pizza in a similar pattern. Add the sweet potato, onion and capsicum.

Using a wide spatula or pizza paddle, gently slide each pizza onto a stone or tile. Cook for 10 minutes. Remove the pizzas from the oven when cooked and golden. Slice each pizza into eight pieces and serve immediately, garnished with the chives.

# Creole Seafood with Roast Peppers & Lemon Chilli Oil

~~~

THIS PIZZA IS FINISHED WITH A LEMON CHILLI OIL THAT IS ESPECIALLY FIERY. BE CONSERVATIVE WITH THE AMOUNT YOU POUR ON UNTIL YOU DISCOVER EXACTLY HOW HOT THIS OIL IS.

### LEMON CHILLI OIL

scant ½ cup (100 mL, 3 fl oz) peanut oil
½ tablespoon sesame oil
1 tablespoon red chilli powder
½ teaspoon black peppercorns
½ teaspoon crushed garlic
1½ teaspoons chopped fresh ginger
½ teaspoon chopped dried lemon grass
grated zest of 1 lemon

2 x 250 g (8 oz) dough balls
  (see page 14)
⅔ cup (150 mL, 5 fl oz) Pizza Sauce
  (see page 16)
1¼ cups (150 g, 5 oz) grated mozzarella
  cheese
100 g (3 oz) scallops, cooked
  (see page 12)
150 g (5 oz) slipper lobster meat,
  cooked (see page 12)
60 g (2 oz) mussels, cooked
  (see page 12)
4 spring onions (scallions), sliced on the
  angle, Chinese style
1 red capsicum (bell pepper), roasted,
  peeled and cut into chunks
  (see page 20)
coriander (cilantro) leaves, to garnish
  (optional)

MAKES 2 MEDIUM PIZZAS

### LEMON CHILLI OIL

Combine the peanut and sesame oils in a small saucepan. Place over a gentle heat until the oil mixture starts to shimmer. Be extremely careful, as the oil may splutter.

Place the chilli powder, black peppercorns, garlic, ginger and lemon grass in a stainless steel bowl. Carefully pour the shimmering oil over the top and let stand for 3 minutes.

Add the lemon zest and let the oil stand for at least 24 hours before using.

This oil will keep indefinitely if stored in an airtight jar or bottle in a cool, dark place.

Place two pizza stones or tiles in the oven. Heat the oven to its highest possible setting (260°C/500°F/gas mark 10). Roll out the pizza dough, as described on page 16, so that you have two bases. Cover the bases with the Pizza Sauce and mozzarella cheese, keeping a 3 cm (1¼ in.) border around the edge of the dough clean.

Distribute the seafood evenly over each base in a clock-style pattern, placing the scallops, lobster meat and mussels alternately. Place any leftover seafood in the centre of the pizza in a similar pattern. Add the spring onion and roasted capsicum.

Using a wide spatula or pizza paddle, gently slide each pizza onto a stone or tile. Cook for 10 minutes. Remove the pizzas from the oven when cooked and golden. Slice each pizza into eight pieces and drizzle a little of the Lemon Chilli Oil over the top. Serve immediately, garnished with the coriander (if using).

# Prawns, Pine Nuts, Pesto & Parmesan

~~~

GARLIC-FLAVOURED PRAWNS (SHRIMP) ARE AN EXTREMELY POPULAR DISH. ENHANCED WITH BASIL AND PARMESAN CHEESE, THEY MAKE A WONDERFUL BLEND FOR THIS PIZZA TOPPING.

2 x 250 g (8 oz) dough balls
(see page 14)
⅔ cup (150 mL, 5 fl oz) Pizza Sauce
(see page 16)
1¼ cups (150 g, 5 oz) grated mozzarella cheese
200 g (7 oz) medium prawns (shrimp), peeled and deveined
¼ cup (60 mL, 2 fl oz) Pesto Sauce
(see page 19)
½ cup (100 g, 3 oz) Parmesan cheese shavings
1 Spanish (red) onion, thinly sliced into rings
2 tablespoons pine nuts
small handful of basil, freshly chopped

MAKES 2 MEDIUM PIZZAS

Place two pizza stones or tiles in the oven. Heat the oven to its highest possible setting (260°C/500°F/gas mark 10). Roll out the pizza dough, as described on page 16, so that you have two bases. Cover the bases with the Pizza Sauce and mozzarella cheese, keeping a 3 cm (1¼ in.) border around the edge of the dough clean.

Place the prawns around the edge of each base in a clock-style pattern. Dollop the Pesto Sauce on each pizza in small spoonfuls. Add the Parmesan cheese and onion rings. Sprinkle the pine nuts and basil over the top.

Using a wide spatula or pizza paddle, gently slide each pizza onto a stone or tile. Cook for 10 minutes. Remove the pizzas from the oven when cooked and golden. Slice each pizza into eight pieces and serve immediately.

# Oyster Kilpatrick

~~~

STRICTLY FOR THE OYSTER FANATICS AMONG US, THIS RECIPE TAKES
THE CLASSIC ELEMENTS OF OYSTERS KILPATRICK AND TURNS THEM INTO
A FABULOUS PIZZA.

2 x 250 g (8 oz) dough balls
(see page 14)

⅔ cup (150 mL, 5 fl oz) Pizza Sauce
(see page 16)

1¼ cups (150 g, 5 oz) grated mozzarella
cheese

10–16 oysters, fresh from their shells

150 g (5 oz) bacon rashers (slices),
without rind, cooked and diced

½ small Spanish (red) onion (about 40 g
(1½ oz)), thinly sliced into rings

40 g (1½ oz) Brie cheese, cut into strips
½ cm (¼ in.) thick

2 teaspoons freshly chopped dill

¼ cup (60 mL, 2 fl oz) Worcestershire
sauce, or to taste

MAKES 2 MEDIUM PIZZAS

Place two pizza stones or tiles in the oven. Heat the oven to its highest possible setting (260°C/500°F/gas mark 10). Roll out the pizza dough, as described on page 16, so that you have two bases. Cover the bases with the Pizza Sauce and mozzarella cheese, keeping a 3 cm (1¼ in.) border around the edge of the dough clean.

Place the oysters around the edge of each base in a clock-style pattern. Sprinkle the bacon over the top of the pizzas. Add the onion rings. Break the strips of Brie cheese into chunks and place on top of the onion. Sprinkle the dill over the top.

Using a wide spatula or pizza paddle, gently slide each pizza onto a stone or tile. Cook for 10 minutes. Remove the pizzas from the oven when cooked and golden. Slice each pizza into eight pieces and liberally sprinkle the Worcestershire sauce over the top. Serve immediately.

# Wok Lobster

~~~

A JAPANESE-INSPIRED COMBINATION OF LOBSTER WITH BLACK BEANS,
PICKLED GINGER, SPRING ONION, CARROT AND CRISPY-FRIED LEEK.
THE PICKLED GINGER IS BEST PREPARED A DAY IN ADVANCE. ONCE
MADE, IT WILL LAST INDEFINITELY IF STORED IN AN AIRTIGHT CONTAINER
IN THE REFRIGERATOR. PICKLED GINGER IS A WONDERFUL CONDIMENT
THAT COMPLEMENTS ANY TYPE OF SEAFOOD.

## PICKLED GINGER

250 g (8 oz) ginger, peeled and cut into
 paper-thin slices
1⅔ cups (400 mL, 13 fl oz) rice vinegar
¼ cup (60 mL, 2 fl oz) cider vinegar
1 tablespoon white vinegar
5 teaspoons caster (superfine) sugar
5 teaspoons salt

250 g (8 oz) slipper lobster meat,
 broken into large chunks
¼ cup (60 mL, 2 fl oz) blackbean sauce
 (available from good supermarkets
 or Asian food stores)
freshly cracked black pepper, to taste
a little peanut oil
a little sesame oil
2 x 250 g (8 oz) dough balls
 (see page 14)
⅔ cup (150 mL, 5 fl oz) Pizza Sauce
 (see page 16)
1¼ cups (150 g, 5 oz) grated mozzarella
 cheese
1 small carrot, cut into fine julienne
6 spring onions (scallions), sliced on the
 angle, Chinese style
2 teaspoons pickled ginger

1 leek, white part only, cut into 5 cm
 (2 in.) lengths and thinly sliced into
 strips
vegetable oil, for deep-frying
salt, to taste
freshly cracked black pepper, to taste

MAKES 2 MEDIUM PIZZAS

### PICKLED GINGER

Place the ginger in a heatproof bowl and
cover with boiling water. Let stand for
2 minutes. Drain. Transfer the ginger to
a large sterilised jar.

Combine the remaining ingredients
in a saucepan. Stir over a moderate heat
until the sugar and salt dissolve. Pour
over the ginger in the jar and seal. Leave
for at least 2–3 hours before using.

Marinate the slipper lobster in the
blackbean sauce. Season with black
pepper. Heat a wok or medium frying
pan over a moderate heat. Add some
peanut oil and a little sesame oil to
the wok or pan. When the oil starts

to smoke, add the lobster meat. Turn to sear on all sides and then remove from the wok or pan.

Place two pizza stones or tiles in the oven. Heat the oven to its highest possible setting (260°C/500°F/gas mark 10). Roll out the pizza dough, as described on page 16, so that you have two bases.

Cover the bases with the Pizza Sauce and mozzarella cheese, keeping a 3 cm (1¼ in.) border around the edge of the dough clean. Place the lobster on each base in a clock-style pattern. Add the carrot, spring onion and pickled ginger.

Deep-fry the leek in vegetable oil until lightly golden and crisp. (If you do not have a deep-fryer, half-fill a saucepan with vegetable or peanut oil, heat gently and cook the leek.) Season with a little salt. Set aside.

Using a wide spatula or pizza paddle, gently slide each pizza onto a stone or tile. Cook for 10 minutes. Remove the pizzas from the oven when cooked and golden. Slice each pizza into eight pieces and serve immediately, garnished with the crispy-fried leek and seasoned with the black pepper.

# Scallops, Asparagus, Crème Fraîche & Almonds

~~~

CRÈME FRAÎCHE IS USED AS THE BASE SAUCE FOR THIS PIZZA. IT RETAINS ITS SUBTLETY AND BLENDS FANTASTICALLY WITH THE OTHER INGREDIENTS. BE SURE TO BUY THE FRESHEST SCALLOPS AVAILABLE.

2 teaspoons butter
½ cup (60 g, 2 oz) sliced almonds
2 tablespoons chopped parsley
grated zest and juice of ½ lemon
¾ cup (200 g, 7 oz) crème fraîche
2 x 250 g (8 oz) dough balls
   (see page 14)
1¼ cups (150 g, 5 oz) grated mozzarella
   cheese
400 g (13 oz) scallops, seared in a hot
   frying pan or skillet until slightly
   undercooked (see page 12)
2 bunches of asparagus, stems peeled
   and spears blanched
extra sliced almonds

MAKES 2 MEDIUM PIZZAS

Melt the butter in a frying pan or skillet over a medium heat. Add the almonds and sauté until they just start to colour. Add the parsley and sauté for a further minute. Add the lemon zest and then the lemon juice. Remove the pan from the heat. Allow to cool and then combine thoroughly with the crème fraîche.

Place two pizza stones or tiles in the oven. Heat the oven to its highest possible setting (260°C/500°F/gas mark 10). Roll out the pizza dough, as described on page 16, so that you have two bases. Cover the bases with the crème fraîche mixture and then the mozzarella cheese, keeping a 3 cm (1¼ in.) border around the edge of the dough clean.

Place the scallops on the bases in a random pattern. Cut the asparagus spears in half lengthways and chop into 4 cm (1½ in.) lengths. Place on the pizzas. Add a few more sliced almonds.

Using a wide spatula or pizza paddle, gently slide each pizza onto a stone or tile. Cook for 10 minutes. Remove the pizzas from the oven when cooked and golden. Slice each pizza into eight pieces and serve immediately.

# Smoked Salmon with Avocado & Brie

~~~

SIMPLE, CLASSIC INGREDIENTS COMBINE TO MAKE THIS AN IDEAL 'BRUNCH' PIZZA. SERVE WITH A LITTLE OLIVE OIL DRIZZLED AROUND THE CRUST FOR A MORE FLAVOURSOME RESULT.

2 x 250 g (8 oz) dough balls (see page 14)

⅔ cup (150 mL, 5 fl oz) Pizza Sauce (see page 16)

1¼ cups (150 g, 5 oz) grated mozzarella cheese

150 g (5 oz) sliced smoked salmon, broken into pieces about 3 cm (1¼ in.) square

1 medium avocado, peeled and quartered, then sliced into crescents

½ small Spanish (red) onion (about 40 g (1½ oz)), sliced

60 g (2 oz) Brie cheese, cut into strips about ½ cm (¼ in.) wide

2 teaspoons freshly chopped dill

sour cream, to garnish

freshly cracked black pepper, to taste

MAKES 2 MEDIUM PIZZAS

Place two pizza stones or tiles in the oven. Heat the oven to its highest possible setting (260°C/500°F/gas mark 10). Roll out the pizza dough, as described on page 16, so that you have two bases. Cover the bases with the Pizza Sauce and mozzarella cheese, keeping a 3 cm (1¼ in.) border around the edge of the dough clean.

Place the salmon on the bases in a random pattern. Add the avocado and onion. Break the strips of Brie cheese into chunks and place on top of the onion. Sprinkle the dill over the top.

Using a wide spatula or pizza paddle, gently slide each pizza onto a stone or tile. Cook for 10 minutes. Remove the pizzas from the oven when cooked and golden. Slice each pizza into eight pieces and serve immediately, garnished with the sour cream and seasoned with the black pepper.

# Barbecue Prawn with Brie & Coriander

~~~

THE BARBECUE IS AS MUCH A PART OF THE IMAGE OF AUSTRALIAN LIFE AS THE BEACH, SO BARBECUE SAUCE SEEMED A LOGICAL PARTNER FOR PRAWNS (SHRIMP) ON THE TOPPING OF THIS PIZZA.

2 x 250 g (8 oz) dough balls
(see page 14)

scant ½ cup (100 mL, 3 fl oz) Pizza
Sauce (see page 16)

¼ cup (60 mL, 2 fl oz) Barbecue Sauce
(see page 19)

1¼ cups (150 g, 5 oz) grated mozzarella
cheese

20–24 medium prawns (shrimp),
cooked, peeled and deveined

125 g (4 oz) bacon rashers (slices),
without rind, cooked and diced

1 medium Spanish (red) onion (about
90 g (3 oz)), cut into wedges and
roasted (see page 20)

60 g (2 oz) Brie cheese, cut into strips
½ cm (¼ in.) thick

½ bunch of coriander (cilantro) leaves,
chopped

freshly cracked black pepper, to taste

MAKES 2 MEDIUM PIZZAS

Place two pizza stones or tiles in the oven. Heat the oven to its highest possible setting (260°C/500°F/gas mark 10). Roll out the pizza dough, as described on page 16, so that you have two bases. Combine the Pizza Sauce and Barbecue Sauce. Cover the bases with this mixture and then sprinkle over the mozzarella cheese, keeping a 3 cm (1¼ in.) border around the edge of the dough clean.

Place the prawns on each base in a clock-style pattern, with two prawns in the centre. Add the bacon and roast onion. Break the strips of Brie cheese into chunks and place on top of the onion. Sprinkle the coriander over the top.

Using a wide spatula or pizza paddle, gently slide each pizza onto a stone or tile. Cook for 10 minutes. Remove the pizzas from the oven when cooked and golden. Slice each pizza into eight pieces and season with the black pepper. Serve immediately.

# Superior Seafood

~~~

A HARVEST OF SEAFOOD WITH DIFFERENT SHAPES GIVES AN INTERESTING VISUAL APPEAL TO THIS PIZZA. TOP IT OFF BY LEAVING TWO OYSTERS IN THE SHELL AND PLACING THEM ON EACH PIZZA AS AN UNUSUAL GARNISH.

2 x 250 g (8 oz) dough balls
(see page 14)
⅔ cup (150 mL, 5 fl oz) Pizza Sauce
(see page 16)
1¼ cups (150 g, 5 oz) grated mozzarella
cheese
4 fresh oysters (plus 2 oysters on the
shell for garnish (optional))
30 g (1 oz) sliced smoked salmon,
broken up into pieces
100 g (3 oz) scallops, cooked
(see page 12)
100 g (3 oz) prawns (shrimp), cooked,
peeled and deveined
60 g (2 oz) mussels, cooked and shell
removed (see page 12)
½ small Spanish (red) onion (about 40 g
(1½ oz)), cut into wedges and roasted
(see page 20)
⅓ cup (40 g, 1½ oz) Parmesan cheese
shavings
2 teaspoons freshly chopped dill
freshly cracked black pepper, to taste

MAKES 2 MEDIUM PIZZAS

Place two pizza stones or tiles in the oven. Heat the oven to its highest possible setting (260°C/500°F/gas mark 10). Roll out the pizza dough, as described on page 16, so that you have two bases. Cover the bases with the Pizza Sauce and mozzarella cheese, keeping a 3 cm (1¼ in.) border around the edge of the dough clean.

Divide the seafood evenly between the two pizzas. Place on the bases in a random pattern, ensuring that the pieces are not piled on top of each other. Add the onion and Parmesan cheese. Sprinkle the dill over the top.

Using a wide spatula or pizza paddle, gently slide each pizza onto a stone or tile. Cook for 10 minutes. Remove the pizzas from the oven when cooked and golden. Slice each pizza into eight pieces and serve immediately, seasoned with the black pepper.

# The Ultimate

~~~

THIS IS A VERY SPECIAL PIZZA MADE WITH PREMIUM SMOKED SALMON AND TOPPED WITH SALMON ROE AND CRÈME FRAÎCHE. PLACE THE SALMON ON THE PIZZA PARTWAY THROUGH COOKING SO THAT IT IS ONLY SLIGHTLY WARMED AND RETAINS ITS DELICATE FLAVOUR.

2 x 250 g (8 oz) dough balls (see page 14)

⅔ cup (150 mL, 5 fl oz) Pizza Sauce (see page 16)

1¼ cups (150 g, 5 oz) grated mozzarella cheese

1 Spanish (red) onion, thinly sliced into rings

1 tablespoon small capers, rinsed of any salt or brine

½ bunch of dill, freshly chopped

200 g (7 oz) sliced smoked salmon

a little extra virgin olive oil

scant 1 cup (200 mL, 7 fl oz) crème fraîche

60 g (2 oz) salmon roe caviar or sevruga caviar

2 dill sprigs, to garnish

freshly cracked black pepper, to taste

MAKES 2 MEDIUM PIZZAS

OPPOSITE: *The Ultimate (top) and Superior Seafood (bottom; see page 105).*

Place two pizza stones or tiles in the oven. Heat the oven to its highest possible setting (260°C/500°F/gas mark 10). Roll out the pizza dough, as described on page 16, so that you have two bases. Cover the bases with the Pizza Sauce and mozzarella cheese, keeping a 3 cm (1¼ in.) border around the edge of the dough clean.

Place the onion on the bases in a random pattern, reserving some for later use. Add some capers. Sprinkle the dill over the top. Using a wide spatula or pizza paddle, gently slide each pizza onto a stone or tile. Cook for 7 minutes. Remove the pizzas from the oven and lay the salmon out over each base so that as much surface area as possible is covered. Place a few more onion rings on top of the salmon. Return to the oven and cook for a further 3–4 minutes.

Remove the pizzas from the oven and drizzle generously with the extra virgin olive oil. Slice each pizza into eight pieces. Place a large dollop of crème fraîche in the centre of each pizza. Dollop a large spoonful of salmon roe beside the crème fraîche. Serve immediately, garnished with the dill sprigs and seasoned with black pepper.

# Grilled Tuna with Orange Chilli Oil

〰️

AN INFUSION OF CHILLI AND ORANGE IS DRIZZLED OVER THE CHARRED TUNA ON THIS PIZZA FOR AN UNBEATABLE TASTE. FOR A MORE SPECTACULAR PRESENTATION, GARNISH WITH SOME CRISPY-FRIED RICE NOODLES.

## ORANGE CHILLI OIL

scant ½ cup (100 mL, 3 fl oz) peanut oil
½ tablespoon sesame oil
1 tablespoon red chilli powder
½ teaspoon black peppercorns
½ teaspoon crushed garlic
1½ teaspoons chopped fresh ginger
½ teaspoon chopped dried lemon grass
grated zest of 1 orange

a little olive oil
200 g (7 oz) tuna steaks
2 x 250 g (8 oz) dough balls
  (see page 14)
⅔ cup (150 mL, 5 fl oz) Pizza Sauce
  (see page 16)
1¼ cups (150 g, 5 oz) grated mozzarella
  cheese
2 red capsicums (bell peppers),
  roasted, peeled and cut into chunks
  (see page 20)
4 spring onions (scallions), sliced on the
  angle, Chinese style
¼ cup (60 mL, 2 fl oz) Orange Chilli Oil
rice noodles, crispy-fried, to garnish
  (optional)

MAKES 2 MEDIUM PIZZAS

## ORANGE CHILLI OIL

Combine the peanut and sesame oils in a saucepan. Place over a gentle heat until the oil mixture starts to shimmer. Be extremely careful as the oil may splutter.

Place the chilli powder, black peppercorns, garlic, ginger and lemon grass in a stainless steel bowl. Carefully pour the shimmering oil over the top and let stand for 3 minutes.

Add the orange zest and let the oil stand for at least 24 hours before using. This oil will keep indefinitely if stored in an airtight jar or bottle in a cool, dark place.

Heat a little olive oil in a frying pan or skillet until very hot. Sear the tuna steaks on one side only. Alternatively, sear the tuna on the grill bars of a barbecue or char-grill. Allow the tuna to cool completely before cutting into large pieces.

OPPOSITE: *Grilled Tuna with Orange Chilli Oil*

Place two pizza stones or tiles in the oven. Heat the oven to its highest possible setting (260°C/500°F/gas mark 10). Roll out the pizza dough, as described on page 16, so that you have two bases. Cover the bases with the Pizza Sauce and mozzarella cheese, keeping a 3 cm (1¼ in.) border around the edge of the dough clean.

Place the tuna on the bases in a clock-style pattern, placing any leftover tuna in a similar pattern in the centre of each pizza. Be careful not to overload the pizzas with tuna. Add the capsicum and spring onion.

Using a wide spatula or pizza paddle, gently slide each pizza onto a stone or tile. Cook for 10 minutes.

Remove the pizzas from the oven when cooked and golden. Slice each pizza into eight pieces. Heap a pile of rice noodles in the centre of each pizza (if using). Drizzle a little Orange Chilli Oil over the top and serve immediately.

# A Vegetarian
# HARVEST

THERE REALLY ISN'T ANY VEGETABLE THAT CANNOT
BE USED IN CREATING GOURMET PIZZAS. IT IS SIMPLY
A MATTER OF WORKING OUT THE BEST WAY TO CUT
AND PREPARE THE VEGETABLE, AND OF JUDGING
HOW WELL COOKED IT SHOULD BE WHEN THE PIZZA
IS REMOVED FROM THE OVEN. AS WITH ANY
INGREDIENTS USED FOR TOPPINGS, FRESHNESS
AND THE SELECTION OF A-GRADE PRODUCE ARE
OF PRIME IMPORTANCE.

ALSO, THE DIFFERENCE BETWEEN USING FRESHLY
CHOPPED HERBS AND THEIR DRIED EQUIVALENT IS
ENORMOUS. ALWAYS TRY TO USE FRESH HERBS
WHERE INDICATED. THE FRAGRANCE RELEASED FROM
THE FRESH HERB IS UNOBTAINABLE ELSEWHERE.
FRESH IS DEFINITELY BEST.

# Cherry Tomato, Ricotta, Roast Garlic & Pesto

~~~

SIMPLE INGREDIENTS KEEP THE FLAVOURS OF THIS PIZZA BASIC, BUT STILL
TASTY. IF YOU'RE NOT KEEN ON GARLIC, OMIT IT AND ADD EXTRA FRESH BASIL.

2 x 250 g (8 oz) dough balls
  (see page 14)
scant 1 cup (200 mL, 7 fl oz) Pesto
  Sauce (see page 19)
½ punnet (125 g, 4 oz) cherry tomatoes,
  halved
100 g (3 oz) ricotta cheese
1 tablespoon roast garlic purée
  (see page 21)
½ bunch of basil, freshly chopped

MAKES 2 MEDIUM PIZZAS

Place two pizza stones or tiles in the oven. Heat the oven to its highest possible setting (260°C/500°F/gas mark 10). Roll out the pizza dough, as described on page 16, so that you have two bases. Cover the bases with the Pesto Sauce and mozzarella cheese, keeping a 3 cm (1¼ in.) border around the edge of the dough clean.

Place the cherry tomatoes on the bases in a random pattern, leaving spaces for other ingredients to fall into. Dot the pizzas with small teaspoons of ricotta. Add the roast garlic in dollops. Sprinkle the basil over the top.

Using a wide spatula or pizza paddle, gently slide each pizza onto a stone or tile. Cook for 10 minutes. Remove the pizzas from the oven when cooked and golden. Slice each pizza into eight pieces and serve immediately.

# Smoked Chilli, Parmesan Cheese & Roma Tomatoes

~~~

THIS TOPPING TAKES THE AGE-OLD FAITHFUL OF CHEESE AND TOMATO
TO A NEW EXTREME WITH THE INTRODUCTION OF CHIPOTLE CHILLI PEPPERS —
A FIERY REBIRTH OF AN OLD CLASSIC.

2 x 250 g (8 oz) dough balls
(see page 14)
scant 1 cup (200 mL, 7 fl oz) crème
fraîche
1¼ cups (150 g, 5 oz) grated mozzarella
cheese
4 Roma (egg, plum) tomatoes, sliced
into rounds
¾ cup (100 g, 3 oz) Parmesan cheese
shavings
4 smoked chipotle chilli peppers, seeded
and finely chopped (jalapeño or fresh
Thai red chilli peppers may be
substituted)

MAKES 2 MEDIUM PIZZAS

Place two pizza stones or tiles in the
oven. Heat the oven to its highest possible
setting (260°C/500°F/gas mark 10).
Roll out the pizza dough, as described
on page 16, so that you have two bases.
Cover the bases with the crème fraîche
and mozzarella cheese, keeping a 3 cm
(1¼ in.) border around the edge of the
dough clean.

Place the tomato slices on the bases
in a random pattern. Add the Parmesan
cheese. Sprinkle the chilli peppers over
the top.

Using a wide spatula or pizza paddle,
gently slide each pizza onto a stone or
tile. Cook for 10 minutes. Remove the
pizzas from the oven when cooked and
golden. Slice each pizza into eight pieces
and serve immediately.

# Goat Cheese, Broccoli, Pine Nuts & Basil

~~~~~~

THE GOAT CHEESE PROVIDES A GOOD CONTRAST TO THE BROCCOLI ON THIS TOPPING, AND A CREAMY BACKGROUND FLAVOUR. IF DESIRED, YOU COULD EASILY ADD SMOKED HAM OR PROSCIUTTO TO THIS PIZZA.

2 x 250 g (8 oz) dough balls
(see page 14)
⅔ cup (150 mL, 5 fl oz) Pizza Sauce
(see page 16)
1¼ cups (150 g, 5 oz) grated mozzarella
cheese
125 g (4 oz) goat cheese, cut into chunks
2–3 heads broccoli, cut into florets and
blanched
1 Spanish (red) onion, thinly sliced
into rings
1 tablespoon pine nuts
½ bunch of basil, freshly chopped

MAKES 2 MEDIUM PIZZAS

Place two pizza stones or tiles in the oven. Heat the oven to its highest possible setting (260°C/500°F/gas mark 10). Roll out the pizza dough, as described on page 16, so that you have two bases. Cover the bases with the Pizza Sauce and mozzarella cheese, keeping a 3 cm (1¼ in.) border around the edge of the dough clean.

Place the broccoli on the bases in a random pattern. Add the goat cheese and lay the onion rings over the top. Sprinkle with the pine nuts and top with the basil.

Using a wide spatula or pizza paddle, gently slide each pizza onto a stone or tile. Cook for 10 minutes. Remove the pizzas from the oven when cooked and golden. Slice each pizza into eight pieces and serve immediately.

# Napoli

~~~

THE RECIPE IS BASED ON THE TRADITIONAL NAPOLI TOPPING, BUT WITH THE ADDED REFINEMENT OF ROAST GARLIC AND FRESH ROSEMARY. THE PERFECT PIZZA TO KEEP THE VAMPIRES AWAY ... AND ANYONE ELSE!

2 x 250 g (8 oz) dough balls
  (see page 14)
⅔ cup (150 mL, 5 fl oz) Pizza Sauce
  (see page 16)
2 cups (250 g, 8 oz) mozzarella cheese
400 g (13 oz) tomatoes, roasted and cut
  into quarters lengthways if necessary
  (see page 20)
1½ tablespoons roast garlic purée
  (see page 21)
½ bunch of fresh rosemary, stems
  discarded and leaves chopped
freshly cracked black pepper, to taste

MAKES 2 MEDIUM PIZZAS

Place two pizza stones or tiles in the oven. Heat the oven to its highest possible setting (260°C/500°F/gas mark 10). Roll out the pizza dough, as described on page 16, so that you have two bases. Cover the bases with the Pizza Sauce and 1¼ cups (150 g, 5 oz) of the mozzarella cheese, keeping a 3 cm (1¼ in.) border around the edge of the dough clean. Reserve the remaining cheese.

Place the roast tomato on the bases in a clock-style pattern, placing a couple of pieces in the centre of each base. Top with the extra mozzarella cheese. Add the roast garlic (if you want a really good garlic 'fix' then use as much as you like). Sprinkle the rosemary over the top.

Using a wide spatula or pizza paddle, gently slide each pizza onto a stone or tile. Cook for 10 minutes. Remove the pizzas from the oven when cooked and golden. Slice each pizza into eight pieces and serve immediately, seasoned with the black pepper.

# Cheeseaholic

~~~~~

FOR THOSE AMONG US WHO ABSOLUTELY ADORE CHEESE. THE FIVE CHEESES USED GIVE THIS PIZZA A SHARP YET CREAMY TEXTURE. SPINACH BALANCES THE OVERPOWERING NATURE OF THE CHEESE, GIVING A MORE ROUNDED FLAVOUR.

## SPINACH PURÉE
a little oil
½ brown (yellow) onion, diced
scant ½ cup (100 mL, 3 fl oz) thickened
   (double, whipping) cream
pinch of nutmeg
½ bunch of spinach, rinsed and stems
   discarded

2 x 250 g (8 oz) dough balls
   (see page 14)
⅔ cup (150 mL, 5 fl oz) Pizza Sauce
   (see page 16)
1¼ cups (150 g, 5 oz) grated mozzarella
   cheese
60 g (2 oz) goat cheese, broken
   into pieces
60 g (2 oz) blue cheese, broken
   into pieces
60 g (2 oz) Brie cheese, cut into slices
   ½ cm (¼ in.) thick
2–3 tablespoons chopped walnuts
   (optional)
½ cup (60 g, 2 oz) Parmesan cheese
   shavings
a few spinach leaves (optional)
chives, finely chopped, to garnish

MAKES 2 MEDIUM PIZZAS

## SPINACH PURÉE
Heat a little oil in a small saucepan. Add the onion and sauté until transparent. Add the cream and nutmeg. Bring to the boil and add the spinach. Mix thoroughly and remove from the heat. Place the spinach mixture in an electric blender or food processor. Blend into a smooth purée and allow to cool before using.

Place two pizza stones or tiles in the oven. Heat the oven to its highest possible setting (260°C/500°F/gas mark 10). Roll out the pizza dough, as described on page 16, so that you have two bases. Cover the bases with the Pizza Sauce and mozzarella cheese, keeping a 3 cm (1¼ in.) border around the edge of the dough clean.

Place small spoonfuls of the spinach purée all over the bases. Add the goat, blue and Brie cheeses in a random pattern. Sprinkle with the walnuts (if using). Add the Parmesan cheese. Garnish with the spinach leaves (if using).

Using a wide spatula or pizza paddle, gently slide each pizza onto a stone or tile. Cook for 10 minutes. Remove from the oven when cooked and golden. Slice each pizza into eight pieces. Serve immediately, garnished with the chives.

# Olive

THIS PIZZA IS FOR THE OLIVE LOVERS AMONG US. SEEK OUT THE
BEST-QUALITY MARINATED, UNPITTED OLIVES FROM YOUR LOCAL
DELICATESSEN FOR THIS RECIPE. THEY HAVE MORE FLAVOUR THAN THE
BOTTLED, COMMERCIALLY CORED VARIETIES.

2 x 250 g (8 oz) dough balls
 (see page 14)
⅔ cup (150 mL, 5 fl oz) Pizza Sauce
 (see page 16)
1¾ cups (200 g, 7 oz) grated mozzarella
 cheese
¼ cup (60 mL, 2 fl oz) olive purée
 (available from good delicatessens)
150 g (5 oz) tomatoes, roasted
 (see page 20)
1 Spanish (red) onion, cut into wedges
 and roasted (see page 20)
⅓ cup (60 g, 2 oz) kalamata olives,
 pitted and cut into quarters
⅓ cup (60 g, 2 oz) green olives, pitted
 and cut into quarters

MAKES 2 MEDIUM PIZZAS

Place two pizza stones or tiles in the
oven. Heat the oven to its highest possible
setting (260°C/500°F/gas mark 10).
Roll out the pizza dough, as described
on page 16, so that you have two bases.
Cover the bases with the Pizza Sauce and
1¼ cups (150 g, 5 oz) of the mozzarella
cheese, keeping a 3 cm (1¼ in.) border
around the edge of the dough clean.
Reserve the remaining cheese.

Dot the olive purée in small portions
(about ½ teaspoon) all over the bases.
Add the roast tomato and roast onion.
Scatter the kalamata and green olives
over the top. Top with the extra
mozzarella cheese.

Using a wide spatula or pizza paddle,
gently slide each pizza onto a stone or
tile. Cook for 10 minutes. Remove the
pizzas from the oven when cooked and
golden. Slice each pizza into eight pieces
and serve immediately.

# Pesto

〜〜〜

THIS TOPPING IS SIMPLICITY IN ITSELF — 'THE' CLASSIC PIZZA.
BASIL, GARLIC, PINE NUTS AND SPANISH ONION ARE BLENDED TOGETHER AND
SMOTHERED OVER THE BASE, AND THEN TOPPED WITH EXTRA CHEESE.

2 x 250 g (8 oz) dough balls
  (see page 14)
scant 1 cup (200 mL, 7 fl oz) Pesto
  Sauce (see page 19)
1¼ cups (150 g, 5 oz) grated mozzarella
  cheese
¾ cup (100 g, 3 oz) Parmesan cheese
  shavings
1 large Spanish (red) onion, thinly
  sliced into rings
1 tablespoon pine nuts
½ bunch of basil, freshly chopped
freshly cracked black pepper, to taste

MAKES 2 MEDIUM PIZZAS

Place two pizza stones or tiles in the
oven. Heat the oven to its highest possible
setting (260°C/500°F/gas mark 10).
Roll out the pizza dough, as described
on page 16, so that you have two bases.
Cover the bases with the Pesto Sauce
and mozzarella cheese, keeping a 3 cm
(1¼ in.) border around the edge of the
dough clean.

Lay the Parmesan cheese on the bases.
Top with plenty of onion rings. Sprinkle
with the pine nuts and basil.

Using a wide spatula or pizza paddle,
gently slide each pizza onto a stone or
tile. Cook for 10 minutes. Remove the
pizzas from the oven when cooked and
golden. Slice each pizza into eight pieces
and serve immediately, seasoned with the
black pepper.

# Tomato, Goat Cheese & Olives with Pesto

~~~

THE SIMPLE, ROBUST FLAVOURS OF TOMATO, GOAT CHEESE AND OLIVES CHARACTERISE THIS PIZZA.

2 x 250 g (8 oz) dough balls
  (see page 14)
⅔ cup (150 mL, 5 fl oz) Pizza Sauce
  (see page 16)
2 Roma (egg, plum) tomatoes, sliced
  into rounds
scant ½ cup (100 mL, 3 fl oz) Pesto
  Sauce (see page 19)
1½ tablespoons kalamata olives, pitted
  and cut into quarters
125 g (4 oz) goat cheese, cut into chunks
½ bunch of basil, freshly chopped
freshly cracked black pepper, to taste

MAKES 2 MEDIUM PIZZAS

Place two pizza stones or tiles in the oven. Heat the oven to its highest possible setting (260°C/500°F/gas mark 10). Roll out the pizza dough, as described on page 16, so that you have two bases. Cover the bases with the Pizza Sauce and mozzarella cheese, keeping a 3 cm (1¼ in.) border around the edge of the dough clean.

Place the tomato slices on the bases in a clock-style pattern, placing two pieces in the centre of each base. Using a teaspoon, place small amounts of the Pesto Sauce in between the tomato slices. Add the olives and goat cheese. Sprinkle the basil generously over the top.

Using a wide spatula or pizza paddle, gently slide each pizza onto a stone or tile. Cook for 10 minutes. Remove the pizzas from the oven when cooked and golden. Slice each pizza into eight pieces and serve immediately, seasoned with the black pepper.

# Triple Tomato with Lemon Thyme

~~~

THIS IS ESSENTIALLY A 'RED' PIZZA. IT HAS THREE DIFFERENT TYPES OF TOMATO ON ITS TOPPING — SUN-DRIED, ROASTED AND CHERRY — ALL TOPPED WITH A TANGY CHEDDAR CHEESE.

2 x 250 g (8 oz) dough balls
(see page 14)
⅔ cup (150 mL, 5 fl oz) Pizza Sauce
(see page 16)
1¼ cups (150 g, 5 oz) grated mozzarella
cheese
½ cup (30 g, 1 oz) sun-dried tomatoes
(drained of oil), diced
250 g (8 oz) tomatoes, roasted
(see page 20)
1 red capsicum (bell pepper), roasted
and cut into chunks (see page 20)
½ punnet (125 g, 4 oz) cherry tomatoes,
halved
½ cup (60 g, 2 oz) grated cheddar cheese
½ bunch of lemon thyme leaves,
chopped

MAKES 2 MEDIUM PIZZAS

Place two pizza stones or tiles in the oven. Heat the oven to its highest possible setting (260°C/500°F/gas mark 10). Roll out the pizza dough, as described on page 16, so that you have two bases. Cover the bases with the Pizza Sauce and mozzarella cheese, keeping a 3 cm (1¼ in.) border around the edge of the dough clean.

Arrange the sun-dried tomato on the bases first. Place the roast tomatoes on the bases in a clock-style pattern, placing two tomatoes in the middle of each base. Add the capsicum and cherry tomato. Top with the cheddar cheese. Sprinkle the lemon thyme over the top.

Using a wide spatula or pizza paddle, gently slide each pizza onto a stone or tile. Cook for 10 minutes. Remove the pizzas from the oven when cooked and golden. Slice each pizza into eight pieces and serve immediately.

# Spinach, Broccoli & Chilli Cream Cheese

~~~

THE UNIQUE BASE SAUCE OF CHILLI CREAM CHEESE MAKES THIS PIZZA ESPECIALLY DELICIOUS. THE OTHER TOPPING INGREDIENTS SINK INTO THE CREAM CHEESE AND PERMEATE IT WITH EVEN MORE FLAVOUR.

## CHILLI CREAM CHEESE

150 g (5 oz) fromage blanc or other soft, fresh cream cheese

juice of 1 lemon

1 teaspoon chilli paste

2 x 250 g (8 oz) dough balls (see page 14)

1¼ cups (150 g, 5 oz) grated mozzarella cheese

2 heads of broccoli, cut into florets and blanched

1 red capsicum (bell pepper), diced

12 button mushrooms, sliced

1 Spanish (red) onion, thinly sliced into rings

extra mozzarella cheese, grated (optional)

16 baby spinach leaves, rubbed with a little olive oil

MAKES 2 MEDIUM PIZZAS

## CHILLI CREAM CHEESE

Thoroughly combine the fromage blanc, lemon juice and chilli paste. This mixture forms the base sauce for this pizza.

Place two pizza stones or tiles in the oven. Heat the oven to its highest possible setting (260°C/500°F/gas mark 10). Roll out the pizza dough, as described on page 16, so that you have two bases. Cover the bases with the Chilli Cream Cheese and mozzarella cheese, keeping a 3 cm (1¼ in.) border around the edge of the dough clean.

Place the broccoli on the bases in a random pattern, leaving spaces for other ingredients to fall into. Add the capsicum, mushrooms and onion. Sprinkle a little extra mozzarella cheese over the top (if using). Add the spinach leaves.

Using a wide spatula or pizza paddle, gently slide each pizza onto a stone or tile. Cook for 10 minutes. Remove the pizzas from the oven when cooked and golden. Slice each pizza into eight pieces and serve immediately.

# Roast Vegetables with Goat Cheese & Basil

~~~

OUR ORIGINAL VEGETARIAN PIZZA, WHICH STARTED LIFE AS LEFTOVERS FROM A ROAST DINNER. ONE DAY I USED LEFTOVER ROAST VEGETABLES ON A PIZZA BASE AT HOME — A SPONTANEOUS IDEA THAT'S BECOME A FIRM FAVOURITE.

1 large eggplant (aubergine), cut into slices ½ cm (¼ in.) thick
1 medium sweet potato or kumara, cut into slices ½ cm (¼ in.) thick
a little oil
salt and freshly ground black pepper, to taste
2 x 250 g (8 oz) dough balls (see page 14)
⅔ cup (150 mL, 5 fl oz) Pizza Sauce (see page 16)
1¼ cups (150 g, 5 oz) grated mozzarella cheese
½ cup (30 g, 1 oz) sun-dried tomatoes (drained of oil), diced
2 tablespoons roast garlic purée (see page 21)
60 g (2 oz) goat cheese, cut into chunks
½ bunch of basil leaves, chopped

MAKES 2 MEDIUM PIZZAS

Preheat the oven to 160°C (325°F/gas mark 3). Place the eggplant and sweet potato on a lightly oiled tray. Season with salt and pepper. Cover the tray with baking parchment. Roast in the oven for 12–15 minutes, or until cooked. Allow to cool. Cut the slices into quarters.

Place two pizza stones or tiles in the oven. Heat the oven to its highest possible setting (260°C/500°F/gas mark 10). Roll out the pizza dough, as described on page 16, so that you have two bases. Cover the bases with the Pizza Sauce and mozzarella cheese, keeping a 3 cm (1¼ in.) border around the edge of the dough clean.

Place the sun-dried tomatoes on the bases. Place the eggplant and sweet potato on the bases in a random pattern. Dot the roast garlic on in very small spoonfuls. Add the goat cheese. Sprinkle the basil over the top.

Using a wide spatula or pizza paddle, gently slide each pizza onto a stone or tile. Cook for 10 minutes. Remove the pizzas from the oven when cooked and golden. Slice each pizza into eight pieces and serve immediately.

# Vegetarian

~~~~~~

A VARIATION OF ITS PREDECESSOR, ROAST VEGETABLES WITH GOAT CHEESE
AND BASIL, BUT WITHOUT THE GARLIC. AN EQUALLY TASTY PIZZA NONETHELESS.

1 large eggplant (aubergine), cut into
   slices ½ cm (¼ in.) thick
1 medium sweet potato or kumara, cut
   into slices ½ cm (¼ in.) thick
a little oil
salt and freshly ground black pepper,
   to taste
2 x 250 g (8 oz) dough balls
   (see page 14)
⅔ cup (150 mL, 5 fl oz) Pizza Sauce
   (see page 16)
1 Spanish (red) onion, cut into wedges
   and roasted (see page 20)
½ punnet (125 g, 4 oz) cherry tomatoes,
   halved
75 g (2½ oz) goat cheese, cut into chunks
½ bunch of basil leaves, chopped
freshly cracked black pepper, to taste

MAKES 2 MEDIUM PIZZAS

Preheat the oven to 160°C (325°F/
gas mark 3). Place the eggplant and
sweet potato on a lightly oiled tray.
Season with salt and pepper. Cover
the tray with baking parchment. Roast in
the oven for 12–15 minutes, or until
cooked. Allow to cool and cut the slices
into quarters.

Place two pizza stones or tiles in the
oven. Heat the oven to its highest possible
setting (260°C/500°F/gas mark 10).
Roll out the pizza dough, as described
on page 16, so that you have two bases.
Cover the bases with the Pizza Sauce
and mozzarella cheese, keeping a 3 cm
(1¼ in.) border around the edge of the
dough clean.

When topping this pizza, be careful
not to stack one ingredient on top of the
other. Place the sweet potato on the bases
in a random pattern. Add the eggplant,
onion, cherry tomatoes and goat cheese.
Sprinkle the basil over the top.

Using a wide spatula or pizza paddle,
gently slide each pizza onto a stone or
tile. Cook for 10 minutes. Remove the
pizzas from the oven when cooked and
golden. Slice each pizza into eight pieces
and serve immediately, seasoned with the
black pepper.

# Vegetarian Supreme

~~~~~~~~

THIS PIZZA IS MORE MEDITERRANEAN IN FLAVOUR THAN THE VEGETARIAN,
WITH ARTICHOKES REPLACING THE SWEET POTATO. SUN-DRIED TOMATOES AND
FETA CHEESE COULD EASILY BE ADDED TO MAKE THIS EVEN MORE OF A
VEGETARIAN EXTRAVAGANZA.

2 x 250 g (8 oz) dough balls
  (see page 14)
⅔ cup (150 mL, 5 fl oz) Pizza Sauce
  (see page 16)
1¼ cups (150 g, 5 oz) grated mozzarella
  cheese
150 g (5 oz) tomatoes, roasted
  (see page 20)
1 red capsicum (bell pepper), roasted
  and cut into chunks (see page 20)
2 globe artichokes, halved then cut into
  quarters
6 button mushrooms, sliced and rubbed
  with a little olive oil
1½ tablespoons black olives, pitted
  and cut into quarters
1 tablespoon roast garlic purée
  (see page 21)
1 Spanish (red) onion, thinly sliced into
  rings
extra mozzarella cheese, grated
  (optional)

MAKES 2 MEDIUM PIZZAS

Place two pizza stones or tiles in the oven. Heat the oven to its highest possible setting (260°C/500°F/gas mark 10). Roll out the pizza dough, as described on page 16, so that you have two bases. Cover the bases with the Pizza Sauce and mozzarella cheese, keeping a 3 cm (1¼ in.) border around the edge of the dough clean.

Place the tomatoes on the bases in a random pattern. Add the capsicum, artichokes, mushrooms, olives and garlic. Lay the onion rings over the top. Sprinkle the extra mozzarella cheese (if using) over the top to hold the ingredients in place.

Using a wide spatula or pizza paddle, gently slide each pizza onto a stone or tile. Cook for 10 minutes. Remove the pizzas from the oven when cooked and golden. Slice each pizza into eight pieces and serve immediately.

OPPOSITE: *Vegetarian Supreme*

# Margherita

〰️

THIS PIZZA IS PROBABLY THE CLOSEST WE MAKE TO A TRADITIONAL TOPPING AT THE RED CENTRE. IT WAS NAMED AFTER THE QUEEN OF SPAIN IN THE EIGHTEENTH CENTURY, PROVIDING A SALUTE TO THE COLOURS OF THE FLAG.

2 x 250 g (8 oz) dough balls
  (see page 14)
⅔ cup (150 mL, 5 fl oz) Pizza Sauce
  (see page 16)
1¼ cups (150 g, 5 oz) grated mozzarella
  cheese
300 g (10 oz) tomatoes, roasted and cut
  into quarters lengthways if necessary
  (see page 20)
¾ cup (90 g, 3 oz) Parmesan cheese
  shavings
1 Spanish (red) onion, thinly sliced
  into rings
1 tablespoon pine nuts
½ bunch of basil, freshly chopped
freshly cracked black pepper, to taste

MAKES 2 MEDIUM PIZZAS

Place two pizza stones or tiles in the oven. Heat the oven to its highest possible setting (260°C/500°F/gas mark 10). Roll out the pizza dough, as described on page 16, so that you have two bases. Cover the bases with the Pizza Sauce and mozzarella cheese, keeping a 3 cm (1¼ in.) border around the edge of the dough clean.

Place the roast tomato on the bases in a clock-style pattern, placing a couple of pieces of tomato in the centre of each base. Top with the Parmesan cheese. Add the onion and pine nuts. Sprinkle the basil over the top.

Using a wide spatula or pizza paddle, gently slide each pizza onto a stone or tile. Cook for 10 minutes. Remove the pizzas from the oven when cooked and golden. Slice each pizza into eight pieces and serve immediately, seasoned with the black pepper.

OPPOSITE: *Margherita*

# Pear, Gorgonzola & Pine Nuts

~~~

THIS PIZZA COULD EASILY BE SERVED AS A SUBSTITUTE FOR EITHER A CHEESE PLATE OR A DESSERT. GORGONZOLA IS A VERY STRONG, CREAMY CHEESE WHICH MELTS EXTREMELY WELL.

2 x 250 g (8 oz) dough balls
  (see page 14)
⅓ cup (90 mL, 3 fl oz) Pizza Sauce
  (see page 16)
¾ cup (100 g, 3 oz) grated mozzarella
  cheese
1 large, firm pear (such as Packham),
  peeled, cored and sliced lengthways
60 g (2 oz) Gorgonzola cheese, cut into
  chunks
2 tablespoons pine nuts or walnuts

MAKES 2 INDIVIDUAL PIZZAS

Place two pizza stones or tiles in the oven. Heat the oven to its highest possible setting (260°C/500°F/gas mark 10). Roll out the pizza dough, as described on page 16, so that you have two bases. Find a plate approximately 18 cm (7 in.) in diameter and place it face down on one of the bases. Take a sharp knife and run it around the outside of the plate to cut a smaller base. Remove the plate. You should now have a round, smooth-edged base. Repeat with the other base.

Cover the bases with the Pizza Sauce and mozzarella cheese, keeping a 1 cm (½ in.) border around the edge of the dough clean. Arrange the sliced pear on the bases in a clock-style pattern, so that the points of the pear meet in the centre. Add the Gorgonzola cheese in a random pattern. Sprinkle the pine nuts (or walnuts) over the top.

Using a wide spatula or pizza paddle, gently slide each pizza onto a stone or tile. Cook for 8 minutes. Remove the pizzas from the oven when cooked and golden. Slice each pizza into four pieces and serve immediately.

# Deep South

~~~

THIS IS ESSENTIALLY A VEGETARIAN PIZZA, BUT IT ALSO TASTES DELICIOUS
WITH THE ADDITION OF CHICKEN.

2 x 250 g (8 oz) dough balls
(see page 14)

scant ½ cup (100 mL, 3 fl oz) Pesto
Sauce (see page 19)

1¼ cups (150 g, 5 oz) grated mozzarella
cheese

½ bunch of dill, freshly chopped

2 leeks, white part only, rinsed and
sliced

1 cup (60 g, 2 oz) sun-dried tomatoes
(drained of oil), diced

¾ cup (100 g, 3 oz) roast corn kernels
(see page 44) (canned corn kernels can
be also be used)

1 red capsicum (bell pepper), diced

salt and freshly cracked black pepper,
to taste

60 g (2 oz) Brie cheese, cut into strips
½ cm (¼ in.) thick

MAKES 2 MEDIUM PIZZAS

Place two pizza stones or tiles in the
oven. Heat the oven to its highest possible
setting (260°C/500°F/gas mark 10).
Roll out the pizza dough, as described
on page 16, so that you have two bases.
Cover the bases with the Pesto Sauce
and mozzarella cheese, keeping a 3 cm
(1¼ in.) border around the edge of the
dough clean. Sprinkle the dill over
the top.

Steam or blanch the leek until just
cooked. Refresh in icy cold water to
prevent the leek cooking further. Drain
and place in a bowl. Add the sun-dried
tomatoes, corn kernels and capsicum.
Season with salt and pepper. Mix
thoroughly. Sprinkle the mixture over the
bases. Break the strips of Brie cheese into
chunks and place on the bases in a
random pattern.

Using a wide spatula or pizza paddle,
gently slide each pizza onto a stone or
tile. Cook for 10 minutes. Remove the
pizzas from the oven when cooked and
golden. Slice each pizza into eight pieces
and serve immediately.

# Beetroot and Goat Cheese

〜〜〜

THE STRIKING COLOUR AND CONTRASTING FLAVOURS OF THE TOPPING
MAKE THIS A STUNNING VEGETARIAN PIZZA. COLD CUTS, LEFTOVER ROAST BEEF
OR PASTRAMI CAN BE ADDED TO COMPLEMENT THE FLAVOURS.

## BEETROOT RELISH

1 tablespoon olive oil

6–8 baby beetroot (beets), peeled and grated

½ cup (125 mL, 4 fl oz) raspberry vinegar

½ cup (125 g, 4 oz) caster (superfine) sugar

2 x 250 g (8 oz) dough balls (see page 14)

⅔ cup (150 mL, 5 fl oz) Pizza Sauce (see page 16)

1¼ cups (150 g, 5 oz) grated mozzarella cheese

125 g (4 oz) goat cheese, cut into chunks

3 Roma (egg, plum) tomatoes, sliced

20 baby beetroot (beet) leaves

½ bunch of chives, freshly chopped

MAKES 2 MEDIUM PIZZAS

## BEETROOT RELISH

Put the olive oil and beetroot in a small saucepan. Cook over a gentle heat for 5 minutes. Add the vinegar and sugar. Cover the saucepan with a lid and continue to cook gently for 15 minutes, until the beetroot becomes soft. Remove from the heat and allow to cool.

Place two pizza stones or tiles in the oven. Heat the oven to its highest possible setting (260°C/500°F/gas mark 10). Roll out the pizza dough, as described on page 16, so that you have two bases.

Cover the bases with the Pizza Sauce and mozzarella cheese, keeping a 3 cm (1¼ in.) border around the edge of the dough clean. Place the goat cheese and tomato on the bases in a random pattern.

Using a wide spatula or pizza paddle, gently slide each pizza onto a stone or tile. Cook for 10 minutes. Remove the pizzas from the oven when cooked and golden. Slice each pizza into eight pieces. Distribute the baby beetroot leaves over each pizza. (If you are using meat on the pizza, place it on now.) Place a large spoonful of Beetroot Relish in the middle of each pizza. Sprinkle with the chives and serve immediately.

# Garden Fresh
# SALADS

THE FOLLOWING SALAD CAN BE CONSIDERED
ACCOMPANIMENTS TO ANY OF THE SAVOURY PIZZAS
IN THIS BOOK OR, INDEED, ANY MEALS. THEY ARE
SIMPLE TO MAKE AND THE DRESSINGS WILL LAST
FOR SOME TIME IF STORED IN THE REFRIGERATOR.

WHEN RINSING SALAD LEAVES, IT IS IMPORTANT
TO BE GENTLE IN DOING SO. FILL A LARGE BOWL
WITH WATER AND PLACE YOUR LEAVES IN IT. SWIRL
THEM GENTLY TO REMOVE ANY DIRT AND GRIT. IF YOU
HAVE A SALAD SPINNER, USE THIS TO SPIN-DRY THE
LEAVES; OTHERWISE, GIVE THE LEAVES A VIGOROUS
SHAKE AND LEAVE THEM TO DRAIN IN A COLANDER
UNTIL NEEDED.

THERE IS NOW AN ALMOST INFINITE RANGE OF
GOURMET SALAD LEAVES AVAILABLE FROM YOUR
GREENGROCER, SUPERMARKET OR DELICATESSEN.
THIS MEANS YOU CAN CHOOSE YOUR OWN 'TAILOR-
MADE' ASSORTMENT OF MIXED LEAVES OR MESCLUN.
AS WITH ANY VEGETABLES, ALWAYS PICK THE
FRESHEST LEAVES AND HERBS AVAILABLE.

# Caesar Salad

CAESAR SALAD IS A WORLDWIDE FAVOURITE, WITH AS MANY VARIATIONS AS
COUNTRIES IT IS FOUND IN. HERE'S OUR PARTICULAR VERSION OF THIS CLASSIC.

## DRESSING

3 egg yolks
½ teaspoon crushed garlic
2 teaspoons Dijon mustard
3–4 anchovy fillets
2 teaspoons champagne or white wine
   vinegar
⅔ cup (150 mL, 5 fl oz) peanut oil
⅓ cup (100 mL, 3 fl oz) olive oil
salt and ground white pepper, to taste

a little olive oil
1 clove garlic, crushed
4 slices stale bread, cut into dice, or
   ⅓ stale baguette, cut into thin slices
4–5 rashers (slices) bacon, rind
   removed
1 head Cos (romaine) lettuce, cut into
   strips 3 cm (1¼ in.) wide, rinsed and
   dried
½ cup (125 g, 4 oz) Parmesan cheese
   shavings
freshly cracked black pepper, to taste
freshly chopped chives, to garnish

SERVES 4

## DRESSING

Place the egg yolks, garlic, Dijon
mustard, anchovy fillets and 1 teaspoon
of the vinegar in an electric blender or
food processor. Blend or process until the
ingredients turn pale and start to thicken
slightly. Combine the peanut and olive
oils. With the motor running, slowly add
the oil to the egg yolk mixture, a few
drops at a time at first and then in a
steady stream, until all the oil is
incorporated. If the dressing is too thick,
thin out with the remaining vinegar. If still
too thick, add a little hot water. Season
with salt and pepper.

The strength of the garlic and
anchovies can be varied to suit individual
tastes, or even omitted. This dressing will
last for up to 2 weeks if stored in an
airtight container in the refrigerator.

Preheat the oven to 160°C (325°F/gas
mark 3). Combine a little olive oil with
the garlic. Place the bread on a baking
sheet. Drizzle with the olive oil. Bake until
golden and crisp, about 10 minutes. Sit
the bacon rashers on a wire rack with a
roasting pan underneath. (As the bacon
cooks, the fat will fall into the pan,
leaving you with crispy bacon.) Roast
in the oven until crisp. Allow to cool and
break into pieces.

Place the Cos lettuce in a bowl. Add
the Parmesan cheese, croutons and
bacon. Season with the black pepper.
Add just enough dressing to coat the
leaves. Toss through with a pair of tongs.
Serve garnished with the chives.

# Marinated & Roast Vegetables with Baby Leaves, Feta & Olives

A DELICIOUS MIXTURE OF ROASTED AND MARINATED VEGETABLES, DRESSED WITH A SIMPLE BALSAMIC VINEGAR AND VIRGIN OLIVE OIL VINAIGRETTE.

1 medium Spanish (red) onion, cut into wedges

a little olive oil

1 yellow zucchini (courgette), cut lengthways into 1 cm (½ in.) strips

1 green zucchini (courgette), cut lengthways into 1 cm (½ in.) strips

60 g (2 oz) mixed baby salad leaves or mesclun, rinsed and dried

1 red capsicum (bell pepper), roasted, peeled and cut into strips (see page 20)

6 marinated artichoke halves, cut into pieces

6–8 sun-dried tomatoes, drained of oil and cut into quarters

60 g (2 oz) feta cheese, thinly sliced

8–10 kalamata olives, pitted and cut into quarters lengthways

1½ tablespoons virgin olive oil or extra virgin olive oil

½ tablespoon balsamic vinegar

freshly cracked black pepper, to taste

SERVES 2

Preheat the oven to 160°C (325°F/ gas mark 3). Place the onion wedges on a baking tray or sheet. Drizzle with a little olive oil. Roast in the oven for 10 minutes. Alternatively, quickly sauté in a hot frying pan or skillet with a little olive oil until the onion just starts to lose its colour, but remains firm. Set aside.

Rub the zucchini with a little olive oil. Quickly sear on both sides in a hot frying pan or skillet. If you have a barbecue or char-grill, sear the zucchini over the bars to give a crisscross effect. Set aside.

Place the mixed salad leaves in the centre of a flat serving plate, reserving some leaves for garnish. Cut the zucchini and roast capsicum into 4 cm (1½ in.) lengths. Place the zucchini, capsicum, onion and artichokes around the leaves. Add the sun-dried tomatoes and feta cheese. Sprinkle the olives over the top.

Spoon the virgin olive oil and balsamic vinegar over the top of the salad. Garnish with the reserved mixed leaves and season with black pepper.

# Vine-ripened Tomatoes with Goat Cheese & Basil

~~~

TRY TO PURCHASE THE BEST-QUALITY TOMATOES YOU CAN FOR THIS SALAD, WHETHER THEY BE VINE-RIPENED OR, BETTER STILL, ORGANICALLY GROWN. CHOOSE BRIGHTLY COLOURED FRUIT WITH FIRM FLESH. THE GOAT CHEESE CAN BE REPLACED WITH FETA OR BOCCONCINI CHEESE, DEPENDING ON YOUR TASTE. YOU MAY ALSO LIKE TO ADD SUN-DRIED TOMATOES TO THIS SALAD.

2 vine-ripened or organic tomatoes

90 g (3 oz) goat cheese

6 yellow teardrop (pear) tomatoes, halved

½ bunch of basil, sliced into very thin strips (or chiffonade as it is known in restaurants)

5 teaspoons virgin olive oil

freshly cracked black pepper, to taste

SERVES 1–2

Wash the vine-ripened tomatoes very carefully and pat dry. Using a very sharp knife, slice into rounds ½ cm (¼ in.) thick. Lay the tomato slices in a circle on a serving plate. Lay the slices of goat cheese in between the slices of tomato, giving you a layered effect. Place the halves of teardrop tomato around the outside of the serving plate. Sprinkle the basil strips over the top of the salad and drizzle with the virgin olive oil. Season with the black pepper.

# Forest Mushrooms & Spinach with Lemon Thyme & Hazelnuts

~~~~~~

THIS IS A WARM SALAD AND SHOULD ONLY BE PREPARED JUST BEFORE SERVING. THE TYPE OF MUSHROOMS YOU USE IS ENTIRELY UP TO YOU, BUT TRY SOMETHING A LITTLE EXOTIC SUCH AS SHIMEJI, SWISS BROWN, ENOKI OR SLIPPERY JACK MUSHROOMS.

½ tablespoon walnut oil or olive oil

30 g (1 oz) prosciutto or bacon rashers (slices), cut into strips about 3 cm (1¼ in.) long

250 g (8 oz) assorted mushrooms, washed and sliced into thick pieces

1–2 bunches of baby spinach, stems discarded, rinsed and dried

a few sprigs of lemon thyme

salt and freshly ground black pepper, to taste

1 tablespoon coarsely chopped hazelnuts

SERVES 2

Heat the walnut oil in a small frying pan or skillet over a moderate heat. Add the prosciutto or bacon. Sauté gently until it starts to become golden. Add the mushrooms and sauté quickly.

While the mushrooms are cooking, arrange the spinach leaves in a pile on a serving plate. Add the lemon thyme to the mushroom mixture. Season with salt and pepper. Remove the mushroom mixture from the pan and spoon directly onto the spinach. Drizzle a couple of spoonfuls of the juice from the pan over the salad. Garnish with the hazelnuts and serve immediately.

# Mixed Leaf Salad with Baby Tomatoes & Balsamic Vinegar

A SIMPLE MIXED SALAD INCORPORATING BABY SALAD LEAVES AND ASSORTED VEGETABLES. THE BALSAMIC DRESSING WILL LAST FOR SOME TIME IF STORED IN AN AIRTIGHT CONTAINER IN THE REFRIGERATOR.

## BALSAMIC DRESSING

1 teaspoon Dijon mustard
¼ cup (60 mL, 2 fl oz) balsamic vinegar
½ cup (125 mL, 4 fl oz) peanut oil
¼ cup (60 mL, 2 fl oz) olive oil

16 cherry tomatoes
16 yellow pear tomatoes
¼ small cucumber (such as Continental), peeled
200 g (7 oz) assorted mixed baby salad leaves or mesclun, rinsed and dried
handful of bean sprouts
½ handful of snow pea shoots
freshly chopped chives, to garnish

SERVES 4

## BALSAMIC DRESSING

Mix the Dijon mustard and balsamic vinegar together in a bowl. Combine the peanut and olive oils. Whisk the mustard and balsamic vinegar mixture. Slowly add the oil to the mixture in a steady stream, whisking continuously, until all the oil is incorporated. Set aside until ready to use.

Slice the cherry and pear tomatoes in half only if necessary (depending on their size). Slice the cucumber in half lengthways and cut into slices. Place the mixed leaves, cucumber slices, tomatoes, bean sprouts and snow pea shoots in a bowl. Spoon over some of the dressing, just enough to moisten the leaves. Toss the salad using a pair of tongs. Transfer the salad to a serving bowl and garnish with the chives.

# Mushrooms with Buttermilk Ranch-style Dressing

~~~~~~

A HEALTHY SALAD WHERE THE MUSHROOMS RETAIN ALL THEIR NUTRITIONAL GOODNESS. EVEN THOUGH THEY ARE SERVED WITH A CREAMY DRESSING, IT IS DELICIOUSLY LOW IN FAT.

¼ cup (60 mL, 2 fl oz) buttermilk
60 g (2 oz) fromage blanc
1 teaspoon lemon juice
1 small clove garlic, peeled, blanched in
  boiling water for 1 minute and finely
  chopped
1 tablespoon chopped parsley
1 tablespoon chopped basil
pinch of cayenne (red) pepper
125 g (4 oz) mushrooms, washed and
  thinly sliced
1 tomato, sliced
freshly cracked black pepper, to taste
freshly chopped chives, to garnish

SERVES 2

Combine the buttermilk, fromage blanc, lemon juice, garlic, parsley and basil in an electric blender or food processor. Blend or process until smooth. Add the cayenne pepper. Place the mushrooms in a bowl and pour the dressing over the top. Cover and leave to marinate for 30 minutes.

Place the tomato slices around the edge of a serving plate. Spoon the mushroom mixture into the middle. Season with the black pepper. Serve immediately garnished with the chives.

# Roast Pumpkin & Zucchini Salad with Rosemary Aïoli

~~~~~~

A ROAST VEGETABLE SALAD FLAVOURED WITH A GARLIC MAYONNAISE AND TOPPED WITH TOASTED SUNFLOWER SEEDS. ANY LEFTOVER MAYONNAISE WILL LAST FOR AT LEAST 3 WEEKS IF STORED IN AN AIRTIGHT CONTAINER IN THE REFRIGERATOR. WHEN MAKING MAYONNAISE, IT IS VERY DIFFICULT TO MAKE QUANTITIES SMALLER THAN THOSE GIVEN BELOW AS THE BASE WILL NOT HAVE SUFFICIENT VOLUME TO INCORPORATE SUCCESSFULLY WITH THE OIL.

### ROSEMARY AÏOLI

3 egg yolks
1 tablespoon Dijon mustard
2 teaspoons white wine vinegar
2 cups (500 mL, 16 fl oz) vegetable oil
2–3 cloves garlic, peeled, blanched in boiling water for 1 minute and finely chopped
½ teaspoon chopped rosemary
salt and freshly ground cracked pepper, to taste

¼ pumpkin (winter squash), cut into wedges about 3 cm (1¼ in.) wide
1 eggplant (aubergine), cut into slices 2 cm (1 in.) thick
a little olive oil
2 zucchini (courgettes), halved lengthways and cut into 3 cm (1¼ in.) pieces
1 red capsicum (bell pepper), roasted, peeled, seeded and cut into strips lengthways (see page 20)
salt and freshly cracked black pepper, to taste
2 tablespoons sunflower seeds, toasted

SERVES 2

### ROSEMARY AÏOLI

Combine the egg yolks, mustard and vinegar in an electric blender or food processor. With the motor still running, slowly add the oil in a thin stream until it is all incorporated. To thin out, simply add a few drops of hot water. You now have a basic mayonnaise.

Take 1 cup (250 mL, 8 fl oz) of the mayonnaise and return to the electric blender or food processor. Add the garlic and rosemary. Pulse to blend through the mayonnaise. Set aside until ready to use. Store the leftover mayonnaise in an airtight container in the refrigerator.

Preheat the oven to 180°C (350°F/gas mark 4). Place the pumpkin wedges in a lightly oiled roasting pan. Place the eggplant slices in a separate lightly oiled roasting pan. Cover with baking parchment. Roast both the pumpkin and the eggplant in the oven for 10–12 minutes, or until cooked. Meanwhile, heat a little olive oil in a frying pan or skillet. Sauté the zucchini for 3 minutes or so. Remove from the pan while still slightly undercooked and firm.

Remove the skin from the pumpkin and cut the flesh into chunks. Place the pumpkin, eggplant, zucchini and roast capsicum in a salad bowl.

Add 3 tablespoons Rosemary Aïoli (thin with a little hot water if necessary) to the salad. Season with salt and pepper. Toss the vegetables to coat with the dressing. Sprinkle the sunflower seeds over the top and serve immediately.

# Mesclun with Creamy
# Blue Cheese Dressing

〜〜〜

THIS SALAD HAS A VERY CREAMY DRESSING THAT CONTAINS WALNUT OIL.
IF YOU FIND THE WALNUT FLAVOUR TOO DOMINANT, SIMPLY REPLACE THE WALNUT
OIL WITH A VEGETABLE ONE. BE CONSERVATIVE WHEN USING THIS DRESSING;
YOU ONLY NEED TO MOISTEN THE SALAD, NOT DROWN IT.

**BLUE CHEESE DRESSING**
1 egg yolk
1 teaspoon Dijon mustard
1½ tablespoons white wine vinegar
⅔ cup (150 mL, 5 fl oz) walnut oil
100 g (3 oz) blue cheese

200 g (7 oz) mixed salad leaves or
  mesclun
125 g (4 oz) blue cheese, or to taste,
  diced
12 cherry tomatoes
½ handful of snow pea shoots
freshly cracked black pepper, to taste

SERVES 2

**BLUE CHEESE DRESSING**
Combine the egg yolk, Dijon mustard
and vinegar in an electric blender or
food processor. With the motor still
running, slowly add the walnut oil so
that an emulsion forms. Once all the oil
is incorporated, crumble the cheese into
the dressing. Blend or process for a few
seconds until smooth.

Any leftover dressing will last for up to
2 weeks if stored in an airtight container
in the refrigerator.

Combine the salad leaves, blue cheese,
cherry tomatoes and snow pea shoots in
a bowl. Add half of the dressing and toss
through using a pair of tongs. Season
with the black pepper. Add more dressing
only if necessary to moisten the leaves.

# Salade Niçoise

~~~

A VARIATION OF THE CLASSIC SALADE NIÇOISE. THIS SALAD IS EXCELLENT WHEN TOMATOES AND GREEN BEANS ARE IN SEASON.

400 g (13 oz) green (French, string) beans, rinsed
8 cherry tomatoes, halved
1 egg, hardboiled and sliced
90 g (3 oz) feta cheese, diced
8 kalamata olives, pitted and cut into quarters
freshly cracked black pepper, to taste
1 tablespoon extra virgin olive oil
juice of 1 lemon

SERVES 4

Trim the ends of the beans. Steam or boil until just tender, 4–8 minutes depending on the size of the beans. Quickly drain and plunge the beans into a bowl of icy cold water to stop them cooking any further. Remove from the water as soon as they are cold and cut into 3 cm (1¼ in.) pieces.

Place the beans, tomatoes, egg, feta cheese and olives in a salad bowl. Season with the black pepper. Add the olive oil and lemon juice. Toss through the salad and serve.

# Just
# DESSERTS

AS STRANGE AS IT MAY SEEM, WE HAVE CREATED
A RANGE OF DELICIOUS AND VARIED DESSERT PIZZAS
... AND, YES, THE SAUCE AND CHEESE HAVE BEEN
REMOVED. AS WITH SAVOURY PIZZAS, THE ONLY
LIMITS TO THE ENDLESS COMBINATIONS POSSIBLE
ARE YOUR IMAGINATION AND CREATIVITY. NOT ALL
OF YOUR CREATIONS WILL NECESSARILY BECOME
GASTRONOMIC DELIGHTS, BUT THE JOY WILL BE
IN THE EXPERIMENTING.

THE DESSERT PIZZAS IN THIS CHAPTER ARE A
SMALLER SIZE THAN THE REGULAR OR MEDIUM
PIZZAS THROUGHOUT THE REST OF THE BOOK, WITH
THEIR BASES MEASURING 16 CM (6 IN.) RATHER THAN
THE NORMAL 26 CM (10 IN.). IF YOU WISH TO MAKE
A LARGE DESSERT PIZZA, SIMPLY USE THE STANDARD
250 G (8 OZ) BALL OF DOUGH AND ADJUST YOUR
INGREDIENTS ACCORDINGLY.

# Crème Pâtissière

〜〜〜

FOR MOST OF THE FOLLOWING DESSERT PIZZAS, YOU WILL FIRST NEED TO MAKE
A CRÈME PÂTISSIÈRE OR PASTRY CREAM. THE RECIPE IS A STRAIGHTFORWARD
ONE AND THE CRÈME PÂTISSIÈRE WILL LAST FOR UP TO ONE WEEK IF STORED IN
A SEALED CONTAINER IN THE REFRIGERATOR.

2 cups (500 mL, 16 fl oz) milk
½ teaspoon vanilla essence (extract)
4 egg yolks
½ cup (125 g, 4 oz) caster (superfine)
   sugar
½ cup (60 g, 2 oz) plain (all-purpose)
   flour, sifted
extra caster (superfine) sugar

MAKES ABOUT 2½ CUPS
(625 ML, 20 FL OZ)

Put the milk and vanilla in a medium saucepan. Bring to the boil over a moderate heat. Be careful not to let it scorch.

Place the egg yolks and caster sugar in a bowl. Whisk together until pale and creamy. Add the flour and mix thoroughly. Pour the hot milk into the mixture and whisk thoroughly.

Return the mixture to the pan and bring to the boil, stirring continuously. Reduce the heat to low and simmer for 2 minutes. The mixture should now be nice and thick.

Transfer to a clean bowl and sprinkle the surface with a little caster sugar. This helps to prevent a skin forming on the top of the crème pâtissière. Allow to cool. If the crème pâtissière is too thick to spread easily, thin with a little single (light whipping) cream before using.

OPPOSITE: *Apricot and Almond (top left; see page 147) and Banana and Passionfruit (bottom right; see page 148)*
PREVIOUS PAGE: *Poached Pear and Hazelnut (see page 146)*

# Poached Pear & Hazelnut

THE HINT OF LEMON INFUSED THROUGH THE SUGAR SYRUP GIVES THIS PIZZA A SUBTLE BALANCE OF SWEET AND SOUR. IT IS PARTICULARLY GOOD AS AN AFTER-DINNER PIZZA SERVED WITH A STRONG COFFEE OR TWO.

## SUGAR SYRUP
1¾ cups (375 g, 12 oz) caster (superfine) sugar
2 cups (500 mL, 16 fl oz) water
juice of 1 lemon
2–3 slices lemon

4 medium pears (such as Packham)
2 x 100 g (3 oz) dough balls
   (see page 14)
1 generous tablespoon crème pâtissière
   (see page 145)
⅓ cup (40 g, 1½ oz) chopped hazelnuts
double (heavy whipping) cream,
   to serve

MAKES 2 SMALL PIZZAS

## SUGAR SYRUP
Combine the caster sugar, water, lemon juice and lemon slices in a medium saucepan. Bring to the boil and use as required. The cooled syrup will last indefinitely if stored in an airtight container in the refrigerator.

Peel the pears and slice into quarters lengthways. Remove the cores. Place in a medium saucepan and barely cover with hot sugar syrup. Place a sheet of baking parchment or greaseproof (wax) paper on top of the pears. Cover with a lid or plate so that the fruit remains submerged. Bring the syrup almost to the boil. Reduce the heat to a simmer and allow pears to poach until almost soft. Remove from the heat and allow to cool in the syrup. When cool, cut the quarters into slices lengthways. Set aside.

Place two pizza stones or tiles in the oven. Heat the oven to its highest possible setting (260°C/500°F/gas mark 10). Roll out the pizza dough, as described on page 16, so that you have two bases.

Cover the bases with the crème pâtissière, keeping a 2 cm (1 in.) border around the edge of the dough clean.

Lay the pear slices on the bases, starting with a circle of overlapping pieces around the edge of the crème pâtissière. Fill the middle of each base with the remaining slices. Sprinkle the hazelnuts over the top.

Using a wide spatula or pizza paddle, gently slide each pizza onto a stone or tile. Cook for 10 minutes. Remove the pizzas from the oven when cooked and golden. Slice each pizza into four pieces using a large chopping or cook's knife. Serve immediately, accompanied by the double cream.

# Apricot & Almond

~~~

APRICOTS, TOASTED ALMONDS AND DATES, LIBERALLY SPLASHED WITH
AMARETTO, CREATE A MEDLEY FIT FOR ANY OCCASION. THIS PIZZA IS ESPECIALLY
GOOD WITH ICED TEA, ALCOHOLIC OR NON-ALCOHOLIC!

200 g (7 oz) dried apricots
hot sugar syrup, to cover (see opposite)
2 x 100 g (3 oz) dough balls
  (see page 14)
1 generous tablespoon crème pâtissière
  (see page 145)
2 dates, pitted and cut into quarters
2 tablespoons sliced almonds
2 teaspoons Amaretto (optional)
double (heavy whipping) cream,
  to serve

MAKES 2 SMALL PIZZAS

Put the dried apricots in a shallow pan. Barely cover with the hot sugar syrup. Place a sheet of baking parchment or greaseproof (wax) paper on top of the apricots. Cover with a lid or plate so that the fruit remains submerged. Allow to cool. Strain off any syrup and set the apricots aside.

Place two pizza stones or tiles in the oven. Heat the oven to its highest possible setting (260°C/500°F/gas mark 10). Roll out the pizza dough, as described on page 16, so that you have two bases.

Cover the bases with the crème pâtissière, keeping a 2 cm (1 in.) border around the edge of the dough clean. Lay the apricot halves on the bases, starting with a circle of overlapping pieces around the edge of the crème pâtissière. Fill the middle of each base with the remaining pieces. Place the date pieces on the bases, one on each quarter. Sprinkle the almonds over the top. Drizzle with the Amaretto (if using).

Using a wide spatula or pizza paddle, gently slide each pizza onto a stone or tile. Cook for 10 minutes. Remove from the oven when cooked and golden. Slice each pizza into four pieces using a large chopping or cook's knife. Serve immediately, accompanied by the cream.

# Banana & Passionfruit

~~~

ANOTHER EXAMPLE OF CLASSIC FLAVOURS COMBINING TO CREATE
GASTRONOMIC HARMONY. AN ABSOLUTELY LUSCIOUS PIZZA, GUARANTEED
TO KEEP THEM COMING BACK FOR MORE.

2 x 100 g (3 oz) dough balls
(see page 14)
1 generous tablespoon crème pâtissière
(see page 145)
1 large banana or 2 medium bananas
1½–2 tablespoons passionfruit
(granadilla) pulp
3–4 tablespoons roughly chopped
pistachio nuts
double (heavy whipping) cream,
to serve

MAKES 2 SMALL PIZZAS

Place two pizza stones or tiles in the oven. Heat the oven to its highest possible setting (260°C/500°F/gas mark 10). Roll out the pizza dough, as described on page 16, so that you have two bases.

Cover the bases with the crème pâtissière, keeping a 2 cm (1 in.) border around the edge of the dough clean.

Slice the banana on a 45-degree angle so that you have nice, long pieces. Lay the banana on the bases, starting with a circle of overlapping pieces around the edge of the crème pâtissière. Fill the middle of each base with the remaining pieces. Spoon over the passionfruit pulp and sprinkle the pistachios over the top.

Using a wide spatula or pizza paddle, gently slide each pizza onto a stone or tile. Cook for 10 minutes. Remove from the oven when cooked and golden. Slice each pizza into four pieces using a large chopping or cook's knife. Serve immediately, accompanied by the double cream.

# Wild Raspberry & Coconut

~~~

FROM TIME TO TIME I USE NATIVE RASPBERRIES FOR THIS PIZZA. THESE ARE CLOSER IN SHAPE TO THE STRAWBERRY AND HAVE MORE SEEDS THAN THE COMMON RASPBERRY. YOU MAY BE ABLE TO FIND NATIVE RASPBERRIES IN THE FROZEN FOOD SECTION OF A VERY WELL STOCKED DELICATESSEN.

2 punnets (500 g, 16 oz) raspberries
hot sugar syrup, to cover (see page 146)
2 x 100 g (3 oz) dough balls
  (see page 14)
1 generous tablespoon crème pâtissière
  (see page 145)
3 egg whites
½ cup (125 g, 4 oz) caster (superfine)
  sugar
3 cups (150 g, 5 oz) coconut threads
  or shredded (flaked) coconut
double (heavy whipping) cream or rich
  vanilla ice cream, to serve

MAKES 2 SMALL PIZZAS

Put the raspberries in a shallow pan. Barely cover with the hot sugar syrup. Place a sheet of baking parchment or greaseproof (wax) paper on top of the raspberries. Cover with a lid or plate so that the fruit remains submerged. Allow to cool. Strain off any syrup and set the raspberries aside.

Place two pizza stones or tiles in the oven. Heat the oven to its highest possible setting (260°C/500°F/gas mark 10). Roll out the pizza dough, as described on page 16, so that you have two bases.

Cover the bases with the crème pâtissière, keeping a 2 cm (1 in.) border around the edge of the dough clean. Using a spoon, place the raspberries on the bases. Use enough raspberries to make a plentiful topping.

Whisk the egg whites in an electric mixer until firm. Add the sugar gradually, whisking continuously, and then the coconut. You should have a nice thick paste. Place a thin layer of coconut mixture on top of the raspberries.

Using a wide spatula or pizza paddle, gently slide each pizza onto a stone or tile. Cook for 10 minutes. Remove the pizzas from the oven when cooked and golden. Slice each pizza into four pieces using a large chopping or cook's knife. Serve immediately, accompanied by the cream or vanilla ice cream.

# Granny Smith Apple Crumble

~~~

THIS PIZZA IS A VARIATION ON TRADITIONAL APPLE CRUMBLE, ONE
OF THOSE OLD-FASHIONED RECIPES THAT IS A DEFINITE WINTER FAVOURITE.
GRANNY SMITH APPLES ARE DELICIOUS COOKING APPLES, WITH THEIR
SLIGHTLY TART FLAVOUR, AND ARE PERFECT FOR THIS RECIPE. THIS PIZZA,
LIKE ITS INSPIRATION, TASTES EVEN BETTER WHEN SERVED WITH A
GENEROUS DOLLOP OF CINNAMON ICE CREAM.

## CRUMBLE TOPPING

1¼ cups (150 g, 5 oz) wholemeal
  (whole-wheat) flour
⅔ cup (150 g, 5 oz) unsalted butter
⅓ cup (60 g, 2 oz) (soft) brown sugar
⅓ cup (45 g, 1½ oz) sliced almonds
2 tablespoons wheat germ
2 tablespoons rolled oats

2 large Granny Smith apples
a little sugar
pinch of ground cinnamon
2 x 100 g (3 oz) dough balls
  (see page 14)
1 generous tablespoon crème pâtissière
  (see page 145)
1 tablespoon currants
double (heavy whipping) cream or
  cinnamon ice cream, to serve

MAKES 2 SMALL PIZZAS

## CRUMBLE TOPPING

Put the flour in a bowl. Rub the butter
into the flour until the mixture resembles
fine breadcrumbs. Add the brown sugar,
almonds, wheat germ and rolled oats.
Mix thoroughly and set aside.

Peel and quarter the apples lengthways.
Remove the cores and slice into strips
lengthways. Place the apples
in a frying pan or skillet with a little
sugar and the cinnamon. Cook gently
over a medium heat until the sugar
dissolves and the apple has softened
slightly. Remove from the heat and allow
to cool.

Place two pizza stones or tiles in the
oven. Heat the oven to its highest possible
setting (260°C/500°F/gas mark 10).
Roll out the pizza dough, as described
on page 16, so that you have two bases.
Cover the bases with the crème
pâtissière, keeping a 2 cm (1 in.) border
around the edge of the dough clean.

Lay the apple slices on the bases, starting with a circle of overlapping pieces around the edge of the crème pâtissière. Fill the middle of each base with the remaining apple, continuing in the same circular pattern. Add the currants. Sprinkle the crumble mixture over the top.

Using a wide spatula or pizza paddle, gently slide each pizza onto a stone or tile. Cook for 10 minutes. Remove the pizzas from the oven when cooked and golden. Slice each pizza into four pieces using a large chopping or cook's knife. Serve immediately, accompanied by the cream or cinnamon ice cream.

# Macadamia, Pecan & Orange

~~~~~

IN THIS RECIPE, THE DOUGH IS USED TO LINE A PIE DISH RATHER THAN
BEING BAKED FLAT. MAKE SURE THAT YOU CUT THE DOUGH OUT SLIGHTLY
LARGER THAN THE DISH, AS IT WILL SHRINK AS IT BAKES.

2 x 100 g (3 oz) dough balls
  (see page 14)
4 eggs
⅔ cup (150 g, 5 oz) caster (superfine)
  sugar
1 cup (250 mL, 8 fl oz) corn syrup
1 teaspoon vanilla essence (extract)
½ cup (60 g, 2 oz) macadamia nuts,
  roughly chopped
⅔ cup (60 g, 2 oz) pecans, roughly
  chopped
3 blood (ruby) or other oranges, peeled
  and pith removed, cut into slices
double (heavy whipping) cream, to
  serve

MAKES 2 SMALL PIES

Preheat the oven to 150°C (300°F/
gas mark 2). Roll out the pizza dough,
as described on page 16, so that you
have two rounds of dough. Lightly grease
two 10–12 cm (4–5 in.) pie pans. Line
each pan with a round of dough. Prick
the dough all over with a fork and then
cover with baking parchment. Fill each
pie shell with baking beans or rice. Bake
in the oven for 12 minutes or until the
dough is cooked on the bottom. The pie
shells are now ready to use. Increase
the oven temperature to 180°C (350°F/
gas mark 4).

Combine the eggs and sugar in a
bowl. Whisk thoroughly. Slowly add the
corn syrup and vanilla essence, whisking
as you do so. Add the macadamia nuts
and pecans. Combine thoroughly. Pour
this mixture into the pie shells and bake
for 35 minutes, or until set. Remove from
the oven and allow to cool.

Lay the sliced oranges on the top
of each pie in a circular pattern, slightly
overlapping each slice. Slice each pie
into four pieces using a large chopping
or cook's knife. Serve immediately,
accompanied by the double cream.

# Mango & Pink Peppercorn

~~~

A HOT AND SWEET COMBINATION, WITH THE FIERY PEPPERCORNS
KEEPING THE SWEETNESS OF THE MANGO IN BALANCE. A TOUCH OF FRESH
MINT ROUNDS OUT THE FLAVOUR.

2 x 100 g (3 oz) dough balls
  (see page 14)
1 generous tablespoon crème pâtissière
  (see page 145)
2 mangoes, peeled and sliced
½ cup (125 mL, 4 fl oz) puréed mango
  slices
2–3 tablespoons water
1 tablespoon pink peppercorns
  (available in good delicatessens or
  gourmet stores)
4–5 mint leaves, finely chopped
double (heavy whipping) cream,
  to serve

MAKES 2 SMALL PIZZAS

Place two pizza stones or tiles in the oven. Heat the oven to its highest possible setting (260°C/500°F/gas mark 10). Roll out the pizza dough, as described on page 16, so that you have two bases. Cover the bases with the crème pâtissière, keeping a 2 cm (1 in.) border around the edge of the dough clean.

Place the sliced mango on top of the crème pâtissière, layering it from the border inwards. Put the mango purée into a small saucepan. Add enough water to make a thick sauce consistency. Add the pink peppercorns and bring the mixture to the boil. Remove from the heat and add the mint. Mix thoroughly. Spoon the sauce over the mango slices, keeping the edge of the dough clean.

Using a wide spatula or pizza paddle, gently slide each pizza onto a stone or tile. Cook for 10 minutes. Remove the pizzas from the oven when cooked and golden. Slice each pizza into four pieces using a large chopping or cook's knife. Serve immediately, accompanied by the double cream.

# Mango, Ginger & Lime

~~~

A TROPICAL BLEND OF MANGO AND LIME, WITH THE GINGER ADDING
A TOUCH OF ORIENTAL FLAVOUR. THIS PIZZA PROVIDES A NOT-SO-SWEET
DESSERT ALTERNATIVE.

2 limes
sugar syrup, to cover (see page 146)
2 x 100 g (3 oz) dough balls
  (see page 14)
1 generous tablespoon crème pâtissière
  (see page 145)
2 mangoes, peeled and sliced
small piece of ginger, peeled and finely
  grated
double (heavy whipping) cream,
  to serve

MAKES 2 SMALL PIZZAS

Remove the zest from the limes with
a zester or peel with a sharp knife. Slice
the zest into very thin strips. Reserve the
lime flesh for another use. Blanch the zest
in fresh boiling water 5 times before
using. This opens the pores of the zest,
removing the bitter acids and allowing
the sugar to penetrate. Place the zest in
a small saucepan and cover with sugar
syrup. Bring to the boil and simmer
gently until the zest starts to become

transparent, 30–40 minutes depending
on the thickness of the zest. Allow the
candied lime to cool in the syrup.

Place two pizza stones or tiles in the
oven. Heat the oven to its highest possible
setting (260°C/500°F/gas mark 10).
Roll out the pizza dough, as described
on page 16, so that you have two bases.
Cover the bases with the crème
pâtissière, keeping a 2 cm (1 in.) border
around the edge of the dough clean.

Place the sliced mango on top of the
crème pâtissière, layering it from the
border inwards. Sprinkle the ginger over
the mango, in moderation. Take some
strips of candied lime and place on top of
the ginger (it does not matter if some of
the syrup goes onto the pizzas as well).

Using a wide spatula or pizza paddle,
gently slide each pizza onto a stone or
tile. Cook for 10 minutes. Remove the
pizzas from the oven when cooked and
golden. Slice each pizza into four pieces
using a large chopping or cook's knife.
Serve immediately, accompanied by the
double cream.

# Rhubarb & Apple

〜〜〜

A 'COMFORT' PIZZA WHICH REMINDS ME OF EATING RHUBARB IN MY MOTHER'S
KITCHEN WHEN I WAS A CHILD. COVER WITH THE CRUMBLE TOPPING ON PAGE 150
TO TRANSFORM THIS PIZZA INTO A MEMORABLE DESSERT PIE.

1 large Granny Smith apple, peeled,
  quartered and chopped into pieces
3 stalks rhubarb, peeled and cut into
  5 cm (2 in.) pieces
pinch of ground cinnamon
hot sugar syrup, to cover (see page 146)
2 x 100 g (3 oz) dough balls
  (see page 14)
1 generous tablespoon crème pâtissière
  (see page 145)
double (heavy whipping) cream,
  to serve

MAKES 2 SMALL PIZZAS

Put the rhubarb and apple into a medium saucepan. Cover with the hot sugar syrup and add the cinnamon. Place a sheet of baking parchment or greaseproof (wax) paper on top of the apple and rhubarb. Cover with a lid or plate so that the fruit remains submerged. Bring almost to the boil, then reduce the heat to a simmer. Poach gently until the apple has softened. Strain off any syrup and allow the mixture to cool in a strainer. The rhubarb should be broken up through the apple.

Place two pizza stones or tiles in the oven. Heat the oven to its highest possible setting (260°C/500°F/gas mark 10). Roll out the pizza dough, as described on page 16, so that you have two bases. Cover the bases with the crème pâtissière, keeping a 2 cm (1 in.) border around the edge of the dough clean.

Spoon the apple and rhubarb mixture over the crème pâtissière. Use enough mixture to give a plentiful topping.

Using a wide spatula or pizza paddle, gently slide each pizza onto a stone or tile. Cook for 10 minutes. Remove the pizzas from the oven when cooked and golden. Slice each pizza into four pieces using a large chopping or cook's knife. Serve immediately, accompanied by the double cream.

# Tofu, Banana & Chocolate

ONCE AGAIN, THIS RECIPE IS FOR A PIE RATHER THAN A FLAT PIZZA. DON'T BE PUT OFF BY THE TOFU IN THIS MOUTHWATERING PIE. ONCE YOU'VE TRIED IT, YOU'LL FIND IT IRRESISTIBLE.

2 x 100 g (3 oz) dough balls
  (see page 14)
200 g (7 oz) cottage cheese
200 g (7 oz) firm tofu (bean curd)
¼ cup (60 mL, 2 fl oz) honey
1 banana, mashed
juice of ½ lemon
½ cup (60 g, 2 oz) plain (all-purpose)
  flour

CHOCOLATE GANACHE
200 g (7 oz) dark (semisweet) chocolate,
  roughly chopped
⅔ cup (150 mL, 5 fl oz) thickened
  (double, light whipping) cream

MAKES 2 SMALL PIES

Preheat the oven to 150°C (300°F/
gas mark 2).

Roll out the pizza dough, as described on page 16, so that you have two rounds of dough. Lightly grease two 10–12 cm (4–5 in.) pie pans. Line each pan with a round of dough. Prick the dough all over with a fork and then cover with baking parchment. Fill each pie shell with baking beans or rice. Bake in the oven for 12 minutes, or until the dough is cooked on the bottom. The pie shells are now ready to use.

Increase the oven temperature to 160°C (325°F/gas mark 3).

Combine the cottage cheese, tofu, honey, banana and lemon juice in a bowl. Stir in the flour and mix thoroughly. Pour the mixture into the prepared pie shells, leaving ½ cm (¼ in.) at the top for the Chocolate Ganache. Bake in the oven for 20 minutes. Remove from the oven and allow to cool. Meanwhile, make the Chocolate Ganache.

CHOCOLATE GANACHE
Place the chocolate in a ceramic or glass bowl. Pour the cream into a saucepan. Bring almost to the boil.

Add half of the cream to the chocolate and stir until the chocolate is partially melted. Stir in the remaining cream and continue to stir until the chocolate is completely melted and the ganache is smooth.

Spoon over the top of the cooled pies and allow to set before serving.

# Calzone of Mixed Berries, Spearmint & Mascarpone

~~~

A FOLDED PIZZA OF SEASONAL BERRIES WITH MASCARPONE CHEESE MAKES FOR A DELICIOUS STUFFED PIZZA. THE MASCARPONE MAY SEPARATE SLIGHTLY WHEN COOKED, BUT THE SUPERB FLAVOUR DOES NOT CHANGE AT ALL.

2 x 250 g (8 oz) dough balls
  (see page 14)
250 g (8 oz) assorted seasonal berries
  (such as strawberries, raspberries,
  blueberries, youngberries, mulberries
  or blackberries)
100 g (3 oz) mascarpone cheese,
  softened to room temperature
8 spearmint leaves, chopped
2 teaspoons chopped nuts (such as
  walnuts, hazelnuts or pistachio nuts)
1 teaspoon coconut threads or shredded
  (flaked) coconut
icing (confectioners') sugar, for dusting

MAKES 2 SMALL CALZONES

Place two pizza stones or tiles in the oven. Heat the oven to 240°C (475°F/gas mark 9). Calzones require a slightly lower cooking temperature and a longer cooking time than ordinary pizzas.

Roll out the pizza dough, as described on page 16, so that you have two bases. Find a plate approximately 18 cm (7 in.) in diameter and place it face down on one of the bases. Take a sharp knife and run it around the outside of the plate to cut a smaller base. Remove the plate. You should now have a round, smooth-edged base. Repeat with the other base.

Place all the berries in a bowl. Add the mascarpone cheese, spearmint, nuts and coconut. Gently fold the mascarpone through the mixture. Brush any excess semolina or flour from the dough. Place half the berry mixture on one half only of each base. Keep at least a 2 cm (1 in.) border around the edge of the dough clean. Brush the border with a few drops of water only. Fold the dough over so that the edges meet. Press together with a fork, ensuring that the edges are completely sealed. Once again, brush any excess semolina or flour from the outside of the dough. Lightly dust the calzones with icing sugar.

Using a wide spatula or pizza paddle, gently slide each calzone onto a stone or tile. Cook for 12 minutes. Remove the calzones from the oven when cooked and golden. Place directly onto serving plates and slice each calzone in half using a large chopping or cook's knife. Serve immediately.

# Index

~~~